THE

COMPLETE

NEW MANAGER

·

**Essential Tips and Techniques
for Managers**

·

EDITED BY JOHN H. ZENGER

New York Chicago San Francisco Lisbon London Madrid Mexico City
Milan New Delhi San Juan Seoul Singapore Sydney Toronto

Available for the first time in one compilation, the material in this book was previously published in *The New Manager's Handbook*, *The Handbook for Leaders*, *How to Motivate Every Employee*, *Dealing with Difficult People*, and *How to Plan and Execute Strategy*.

2 3 4 5 6 7 8 9 10 11 12 WFR/WFR 1 9 8 7 6 5 4 3 2 1 0

ISBN 978-0-07-174447-8
MHID 0-07-174447-9

Contents

PART 1
NEW MANAGER ESSENTIALS

Congratulations on joining the ranks of management. Your hard work has paid off, and now you have responsibility for supervising the work of others to help your organization achieve its goals. While your expertise and success in your work has likely contributed to your promotion to manager, you're probably aware that this new position requires a different set of skills—skills that require effective interaction with other people at work. These people include those you supervise, your peers, and the managers you report to.

There's an old joke that disgruntled employees sometimes tell each other. "You know the definition of manager, don't you?" "No, tell me." "A manager is the person who sees the visitors so everyone else can get the work done." Maybe that's funny to some people, but now that you're a manager, it's your job to laugh *with* your staff, rather than having them laugh *at* you.

At the heart of managing are planning and communication, and you'll find numerous lessons here that deal with the nuances of these skills, including giving feedback to your employees to help them improve their performance and keep up the motivation, how to give great instructions to get the results you're looking for, how to build alliances, and how to listen to others. You need to learn to run meetings that employees know will help them successfully work together; you need to learn how to think strategically as well as tactically; you need to learn how to build alliances. And while you may understand the theory of these things, it's actually doing them that is the issue.

Soon enough, you will no longer be a new manager, but one who clearly understands the nature of your responsibilities and the opportunities you have to make a real difference for your organization and yourself. Good luck!

"In the end, all management can be reduced to three words: people, product, and profits. People come first."

—Lee Iacocca

1

Give Feedback

Part of your job as a new manager is to give helpful feedback to employees. But it doesn't stop there.

The feedback process isn't over when you reel off what you think the employee should do to improve performance. It ends when the worker understands your input and applies it successfully.

Most managers dislike giving negative feedback. They may fear that workers will perceive their well-intentioned comments as personal criticism. And because it's common for rookie managers to want to be liked by their troops, they may shy away from pointing out work-related defects or concerns about an individual's effort or attitude.

Get over it!

Effective managers must give feedback every day. It can range from glowing praise to neutral observation to serious alarm. Ideally, positive input should far outweigh everything else. Employees crave compliments from their supervisor—they remember

them, treasure them, and share them with friends and family.

Look for opportunities to point out what workers are doing right. Don't feel you must ration praise only for rare flashes of brilliance or exceptional results. Letting people know that you admire how they handle a customer, organize their workspace, or analyze a problem is in itself a form of feedback that strengthens your relationship with your team.

When your goal is to provide constructive feedback that helps employees improve, set the stage. Get a two-way conversation going. Discuss the high standards you set for yourself and your crew—and find out what the worker thinks of these standards. That's better than coming right out and saying, "Here's something you're doing wrong that you need to work on . . ."

Remember that almost all workers thirst for input. One of the employees' biggest complaints is "I don't get enough feedback from my boss." Remove the mystery. Freely share your ideas, suggestions, and reservations. Make individuals aware of their performance and guide them to improve.

Use this three-step method to deliver feedback that sinks in:

Invite employees to evaluate their performance: Let them rate a specific aspect of their work based

on, say, a 1-to-10 scale or an A-to-F letter grade. Many people judge themselves more harshly than you would. Even if they inflate their rating, it gives you a baseline to respond with your input.

Ask follow-up questions: Dig for more information. Get employees to share details or examples that justify their self-rating. Notice what criteria they use to evaluate themselves and how they track their performance.

Align your analysis with their comments: Now that you've given employees a chance to chime in, it's your turn. Begin by thanking them for explaining how they view their performance. Then add, "I'd like to piggyback on what you've said." Start by giving feedback that they missed. Then endorse positive input that you heard earlier (as long as you agree) and add some fresh praise so you end on a high note.

"The good ones among managers . . . do not talk to their subordinates about their problems, but they know how to make the subordinates talk about theirs."

—Peter Drucker

2

Make the Best of Bad News

The way you express bad news will make or break your credibility as a manager. If you level with employees, you show that you're a no-nonsense leader who prizes clear communication. But if you talk around the issue, others may follow your example and avoid addressing problems that need attention.

Prepare to deliver bad news. Decide in advance what you want to accomplish by speaking up. Do you want to spur your employees to take action or simply raise their awareness? Is there an upside to the situation and, if so, should you emphasize it? Do you want to discuss the evolution of the problem or limit your comments to the here and now?

Maintain your perspective. New managers sometimes blow bad news out of proportion by "awfulizing" it to the point where it takes on a life all its own. Realize that setbacks come with the territory; take them in stride and convey bad news to others

so they, too, see the situation accurately rather than as Armageddon.

Watch your tone and mannerisms. Speak in succinct, straightforward terms. Give the facts without editorializing. For example, skip phrases such as "I hate to tell you this" or "This is the part of my job I dread most" and jump right to the point.

Don't sigh, shrug, and repeatedly shake your head in dismay. Imagine you're Walter Cronkite reporting the news with an undercurrent of strength and perseverance in your voice. If you start flinching or feeling too overwrought about it, your employees may focus more on your pained demeanor than the news itself.

End on an upbeat note. Set a goal for future improvement or present a strategy that addresses the source of the problem. Left to fester, bad news can hurt morale. Dangle hope or offer solutions to boost employees' attitudes.

Here are three techniques to make bad news more palatable:

Display "ego strength": Show that your ego isn't threatened by the bad news. Use nondefensive language such as, "I take responsibility for contributing to this state of affairs, and I take responsibility for leading us out of this." As a new manager, you can say, "I'm learning every day, so I want you to know what I've learned."

Set the context: Tie a specific piece of bad news to larger organizational goals. Say, "This adds to our challenge, but we can overcome it."

Get to the point: Stay on track and don't waste words. State the most important news up front. Then add facts, evidence, or other supporting information.

"Communicate everything you possibly can to your partners. The more they understand, the more they'll care. Once they care, there's no stopping them."

—Sam Walton

3

Delegate

Effective managers must have faith—in their people. Your success depends on your willingness to rely on employees to take initiative, solve problems, and produce results.

You've surely heard the advice: delegate when possible. But it's not that simple. If you do it the wrong way, delegation can backfire.

Andrew Carnegie said, "The secret of success is not in doing your own work but in recognizing the right man to do it." Delegation thus takes forethought. Match the right employee with a challenging assignment.

Consider an individual's *interests*, *strengths*, and *expertise*—and hand off tasks to employees who rate highly in at least two of those three categories. If you want someone to research and respond to customer complaints, for instance, delegate the project to an employee who enjoys serving customers, possesses excellent people skills, and

knows how to investigate problems and dig for answers.

By delegating, you improve your efficiency. You can focus on high-priority issues and not get bogged down in work that depletes your time and energy. At the same time, you can develop your employees and make them more valuable contributors.

Don't confuse delegation with assigning routine work to employees that falls within their normal job duties. True delegation involves giving someone the responsibility and authority to do something that's normally part of *your* job.

Delegation is not "dumping." If employees think you're tossing the least desirable assignments on their lap, they'll resent it.

Set up controls and checkpoints to monitor your employees' progress. Discuss how you can both evaluate progress and measure a project's success.

Define clear goals and expectations for the assignment. But don't explain how to do it. Let others discover for themselves how to follow through.

New managers often assume that once they delegate, they're no longer accountable for the results. But handing over responsibility and authority to employees has its limits. Ultimate accountability remains with you—whether you realize it or not.

Rookie managers sometimes fall into the trap of taking an assignment back unwittingly. They might say, "Here, let me show you," and they wind up

doing the whole project. Avoid this by letting employees problem-solve for themselves.

Follow these pointers to delegate well:

Step back: Select tasks that employees can control and implement on their own. Make sure the individual can exercise judgment and autonomy. If you micromanage, delegating does more harm than good.

Clarify the assignment: Confirm that employees understand the purpose, the goal, and the performance measures you'll use to judge success. Remove ambiguities and set a clear deadline.

Run an "I'm not here" test: Identify key aspects of your job—and decide who could handle those responsibilities in your absence. By anticipating what you want employees to do when you're not there, you can delegate pieces of your managerial duties to them now so they're ready to step in later.

"Strange as it sounds, great leaders gain authority by giving it away."

—James B. Stockdale

4

Pick the Brains of Departing Workers

When an employee quits, you have a golden opportunity to learn how to do your job better. How? On or just before the worker's last day, schedule an exit interview.

People on the way out the door often speak freely about how they—and their coworkers—view management. All you have to do is ask smart questions and listen.

Invite departing employees to give their opinions about what you and your organization do right and wrong. Take notes. Show interest in their observations and follow up.

Most employees, even embittered ones, will remain civil while sharing information and insights that make you a stronger, wiser manager. Once they see you're eager to pick their brains, they'll usually open up.

Don't assume departing employees will use the exit interview to settle scores with colleagues, unleash their pent-up anger at company policies, or lecture you about misguided change campaigns or management screwups. Asking neutral questions helps. "Can you describe the level of teamwork you've experienced?" is better than "Are you disappointed in our teamwork?"

Assure employees of confidentiality. Explain that you value their input and you want them to raise honest concerns.

Exit interviews can help you identify reasons for high turnover or poor morale, expose poor working conditions, and gain ideas that sharpen how you manage. Longtime workers can reflect on their years at your organization, pointing out pros and cons of various policies, procedures, or personnel. They may know what works and what doesn't—and who are the unsung heroes in your unit. An exit interview is one of the only ways for new managers to gather such valuable insight.

Better yet, your genuine interest in the departing employee's views can leave a lasting positive impression. The individual may come away feeling better about you, and this can work in your favor later. Cultivating allies outside your organization helps you build a valuable network.

To squeeze the most knowledge from departing workers:

Lay the groundwork: Let employees know in advance what you're going to ask. Emphasize that you treat their opinions seriously and you hope they'll give considerable thought to the issues before the interview.

Separate tangibles from intangibles: Ask two sets of questions. First, focus on fact-finding (example: "Did you have the tools and resources you needed to do the job?"). Then shift to less concrete, hard-to-measure areas such as morale and camaraderie (example: "How would you rate the work ethic of your team?").

Request names: Collect referrals for new hires, vendors, and consultants. Probe to find the names of the individuals your departing employees respect most both inside *and outside* your organization. Discuss your hiring needs and invite the employee to stay in touch and refer top candidates to you in the weeks and months ahead.

"Most of the successful people I've known are the ones who do more listening than talking."
—Bernard Baruch

5
Review Performance Regularly

Most employees hunger for information on how they're doing. They want a boss who administers regular performance reviews—and provides a thorough, thoughtful evaluation that's constructive and well supported.

Many new managers dread performance appraisals, especially when meeting with employees with poor or inconsistent performance. What's worse, the review process in many organizations is a burdensome administrative task that requires reams of paperwork.

Formal performance reviews become easier if you informally update employees about the quality of their work throughout the year. If they know on any given day what they do well and what they need to improve, then there will be few surprises during your regularly scheduled appraisals.

Balance strengths and weaknesses when reviewing someone's performance. Don't go overboard in

either direction. If you dwell on employees' defects, you may overlook what they do well and deaden their spirit. But nonstop gushing can lead workers to conclude they can do no wrong in your eyes. Aim for at least a 3-to-1 ratio of pointing out what's right and what's wrong about an individual's performance.

Stick to the facts. Describe performance based on what you've seen firsthand or solid evidence you've collected. Give dates and times to substantiate your observations. Avoid labels like "careless" or "sloppy." Instead, cite concrete reasons *why* you perceive someone this way. One of the hardest lessons for new managers to learn when reviewing employees' performance is to allow the workers to judge for themselves how they're doing—after citing specific examples of their actions.

Strive for accuracy. Unseasoned managers tend to gloss over employees' performance problems by rating individuals as "fine" or "above average" in all categories without much thought. That's risky. If a worker's performance declines to the point where termination becomes an issue, you may lack the documentation you need to prove that person's performance was already shaky at the last performance appraisal.

Here's how to capitalize on performance reviews:

Stick to a schedule: Employees are counting the days until their next review, so honor your commit-

ments. Whether you promise appraisals quarterly, semiannually, or annually, follow through. If you postpone reviews or force employees to nag you because you forgot, you'll kill morale.

Use the DISC formula: DISC stands for "describe impact, specify consequences." When you assess performance, describe the specific behavior, discuss its impact, specify what you want to happen, and explain the consequences—both good and bad—based on the employee's response.

Suggest, don't threaten: Make sure your goal in reviewing someone's performance is to impart knowledge that allows the person to improve. Rather than insist that a receptionist's curt demeanor must stop, focus on how much there is to gain by adopting a more genial manner.

"It's only as we develop others that we permanently succeed."

—Harvey S. Firestone

6

Decide and Deliver

Now that you're a manager, you'll need to make more decisions than ever before. And you will probably wish you had more time, more information, and more guidance before making tough calls.

By developing a system for calm, rational decision making, you'll gain confidence when operating under duress. You can decide quickly and deliver great results without backtracking, dallying, or leading others to question your judgment.

Decisions revolve around three steps: gathering facts, identifying options, and choosing the best one. Relevant facts can come from a range of sources, from employees to customers to activity reports and other quantitative measures.

Listing your full range of possible moves requires an open mind. Options that may seem off-the-wall or foolhardy at first may prove worthy of consideration, perhaps when combined with other alternatives. When deciding among all your options,

you'll want to apply objective criteria to pinpoint the most sensible, effective choice of action.

Delay can wreak havoc on your decision making. Waiting induces stress. It prolongs uncertainty and can lead others to doubt your managerial muscle. Collecting facts and weighing options need not be a long, tortuous process.

If you're facing a series of unappealing options, ask yourself, "What's the worst that can happen?" Evaluate the likelihood of different outcomes and isolate variables you can control. This way, you can weigh the worst-case odds against more acceptable outcomes.

Indecision thrives if you're reluctant to accept accountability for your actions. You may not want to provoke others by making a controversial decision or take a stand that turns out wrong. Or you may be overwhelmed by the complexity or magnitude of the decision—and look for excuses to postpone making it.

Combat indecision by setting a deadline. Force yourself to make the best judgment possible with the facts available within a set time frame.

To communicate decisions that might upset others, use diplomatic phrases such as, "I understand your position, but I have to weigh what's best for this organization" or "There are arguments to be made on all sides, so it's particularly tough in this case to please everyone."

To march confidently toward a decision:

Address ambivalence head-on: Acknowledge uncertainty; don't brush it aside. Examine why you're ambivalent. For example, your gut instinct may conflict with what the facts lead you to conclude. Write down your doubts and view them from a detached, dispassionate point of view.

Create a contingency plan: Devise a backup plan in case your decision turns sour. Prepare to mitigate your losses.

Use best- and worst-case scenarios as bookends: Consider the full spectrum of outcomes, from best to worst. Then take steps that minimize the worst case.

"The fact is you'll never have all the information you need to make a decision—if you did, it would be a foregone conclusion, not a decision."

—David Mahoney

7

Use "Praise Motivation"

There's no mystery to motivating employees. It's all about expressing your sincere admiration for them. When they know that you respect their effort, ability, and work product, they're more apt to enjoy their job and heed your directives.

Genuine praise is the ultimate energizer. Think how much more motivated you've become when bosses have applauded your performance. It's a surefire way to build individuals' confidence and push them to excel even more.

The irony is that while most managers know praise serves as a superb motivator, putting that knowledge to work often poses a challenge. Daily pressures, crises, and mishaps may make it hard for you to feel positive about your employees. It's easy to overlook what they're doing right when what goes wrong demands so much of your time and attention.

Praise can take many forms. You can send non-verbal signals such as a pat on the back, an approv-

ing nod, or the thumbs-up. Or you can drop quickie comments that make an employee's day such as, "Fine work" or "You outdid yourself this time."

There are more subtle ways to praise. For instance, you can ask employees for their opinions. Preface your question by saying, "I'd like to pick your brain" or "You can probably shed some light on this for me." Don't hint what you want them to say. Just listen, and you'll make them feel important.

Another simple motivator is to use employees' names when you chat with them. You'll get off to a great start as a manager if you learn everyone's name quickly and weave it into conversations. Workers respond more enthusiastically when their supervisors speak to them in a friendly, personal tone.

Rookie managers sometimes assume they should ration their praise. Otherwise, they may figure that employees will come to expect it all the time. Yet there's no such thing as too much praise as long as it's grounded in real accomplishment. Whenever a staffer earns your admiration, say so.

Praise works best when it's specific. Expressing gratitude never hurt, but if you explain *why* you're thanking a worker, you heighten the effect. Get in the habit of saying, "Thank you for . . ." rather than just blurting out "Thanks" and moving on.

Better yet, find new ways to communicate your praise. Write a note, send an e-mail card, or give a

small gift or half-day off in exchange for exceptional work. The more you can convey your thanks creatively, the more your employees will strive to earn it.

Master "praise motivation" by embracing these work habits:

Catch employees at their best: Look for examples of stellar work. Set high standards and never miss a chance to congratulate someone for exceeding them.

Acknowledge effort, not just results: Some employees will try—and fail. That's the ideal time to say, "I like the way you tried so hard." Don't just shrug and say, "Oh well, at least you tried" or "Maybe next time." Recognize effort as praiseworthy in itself.

Say it once—with feeling: Praise loses its luster if you repeat yourself too often. Find fresh traits, skills, or actions to compliment. And once you say it, don't keep restating it until the employee's face lights up. Some individuals don't react to praise with visible delight, but that doesn't mean they disregard it.

"There is no verbal vitamin more potent than praise."

—Frederick B. Harris

8

Plan Your Meetings

In most cases, the best meetings are short meetings.

One of the reasons that meetings get such a bad rap is that they tend to drag on too long. That often happens when a few individuals monopolize the proceedings, or the group constantly veers from the high-priority issues.

New managers who aren't accustomed to running meetings may defer too much to attendees. Or they may overcompensate for their lack of experience by playing the tyrant and stifling healthy debate. By preparing well and keeping everyone focused on what counts, you can save time while building consensus or generating buy-in.

Before the meeting, narrow the scope. Craft an agenda that defines a specific problem and seeks ways the group can address it. Don't overload the meeting with too many disparate issues.

Distribute the agenda in advance, along with related data that you want everyone to absorb ahead

of time. That way, you won't waste time in the meeting engaging in information sharing. Make sure the discussion focuses on solutions, not defining the problem.

Set up the room to advance your agenda. If you want to encourage free-flowing discussion, arrange the chairs in a U or circle. If you're eager to reach fast decisions in an abbreviated meeting, remove the chairs so everyone must stand. Fill out flip charts in advance so you don't bore attendees while you do lots of writing.

To rivet the group's focus on the overriding goal of the meeting, write it down and post it on a side wall. Point to it whenever the discussion threatens to head off course as a silent reminder to everyone to stay on track.

Look at everyone in the room when you speak. Don't just establish eye contact with one or two people or you'll risk excluding others. Notice when someone's trying to get a word in. Recognize quiet or shy individuals, and give them ample opportunity to contribute. Welcome questions, but don't hesitate to say "We can answer that later" if necessary.

To make meetings more effective:

Meet and greet at the door: Shake hands with people as they arrive. That's better than arriving early, planting yourself in a chair, looking down, and fiddling with papers as others file in.

Open with an overview: Use the first minute of the meeting to state the purpose of the meeting. Also reveal what attendees will gain by the end. Highlight key agenda items and any planned group activities.

Commit assignments to writing: End the meeting by deciding who will do what—by what date. Misunderstandings will result if you skip this step or assume people know what to do next. Write assignments and send a follow-up memo summarizing everyone's job.

"At Intel, agendas . . . include information about the meeting's key topics, who will lead various parts of the discussion, how long each topic of discussion will take, and what outcomes are expected."

—Michelle Neely Martinez

9

Think Strategically

The past decade has introduced the term "knowledge worker" to the workplace. That likely makes you a "knowledge manager."

Employees at all levels are expected to *think*—to propose ideas and streamline production or customer service so the organization runs better. As a manager, your role is to devise strategic plans and communicate them dynamically to your team. These plans provide goals and direction for how you and your employees can effectively do your work for the organization.

Thinking strategically is a learned skill. You develop strategic savvy by asking smart questions, digging for answers, and looking past assumptions or "truths" that limit your perspective.

You've probably never given much thought to your strategic thinking prowess. It's not an easy-to-evaluate skill, like typing or writing memos. But now that you're a manager, you must demonstrate

your ability to think outside the box and attack challenges with intellectual vigor.

Your bosses will judge you in part on how well you analyze business problems and present creative solutions. They did not climb the ladder by accepting conventional wisdom blindly. By sharing your knowledge and learning from experience, you will impress higher-ups as a strategic whiz.

You need to tap the full range of your intelligence—and the brainpower of your staff—to maximize your contribution. Get in the habit of asking penetrating questions of your staff and giving them the time to research the answers. The more you ask, the more you—and they—will learn.

Running a SWOT analysis helps you think strategically (strengths, weaknesses, opportunities, and threats). Identifying the pros and cons, along with the opportunities and dangers that might arise, enables you to assess how to proceed. Involve your staff in this exercise. Welcome their input and brainstorm freely. This gives everyone a chance to make each other smarter.

Graduate to a higher level of strategic thinking by applying these tools:

Dig down at least three layers: Look deeper than the surface problem. Keep asking "why." You'll know you've examined an issue in depth when you've dug at least three levels down to expose the

inner workings of an issue—the root causes that merit attention.

Perform triage: Separate facts or insights that matter from irrelevant details that you can ignore or file away. Focus only on the most compelling, revealing strands of information to avoid getting buried in a dumping ground of data.

Weigh all sides—and all consequences: Think ahead to identify the repercussions of a strategic decision. Know what's at stake and predict the range of consequences to eliminate nasty surprises later.

"To think strategically is to think with discipline and make informed decisions about the direction you want to go."

—John Woods

10

Build Alliances

You cannot succeed in a vacuum as a manager. You need allies—the more the better.

Yet there's a difference between cultivating friends throughout your organization and being liked by your employees. You should not befriend the people who report to you. Treat them with kindness and respect, but don't expect to socialize with them or confide in them.

Woo allies from among your coworkers and bosses. Seek out folks you admire and get to know them. Exchange favors. Share information. Celebrate joint victories and commiserate over defeats.

Getting people to like you requires tact and sensitivity. For example, while impulsiveness has its place, rushing to say whatever pops into your head almost guarantees that you'll drive away potential allies.

Pause an extra second before you say something even remotely controversial to a colleague. Step

into that person's shoes and imagine his or her reaction. If you're stating an opinion, acknowledge others' views before you volunteer your own. Quote them favorably, praise their actions, and let them know when you've learned from them. As long as you're sincere, you'll attract allies with ease.

Listen for indirect requests for help. If a coworker mentions that he intends to "read up on the new software," offer to give him a quick lesson. If an executive asks you how she can learn more about a recent shipment of parts, offer to gather all the information she needs and have it on her desk in the morning.

Also pounce on opportunities to solve others' problems. When someone expresses frustration, concern, or uncertainty about a business-related matter, lend an attentive ear. If the person has a big ego, you may want to frame your proposed solutions as questions, not statements. Asking, "Have you tried . . ." works better than declaring, "I think you should try . . ."

Spread the word when you admire how someone acts. When a colleague wins an award or a senior executive makes a decision you deem gutsy or visionary, tell everyone from your employees to vendors and suppliers. As the messenger of good news, you'll gain allies when the subjects of your admiration hear how much they've impressed you.

Congratulate individuals on their achievements. If a coworker earns a professional designation or tells you that his son won a college scholarship, offer to host an office party. Your selfless attention to others will not only brighten their day but also make your job easier as allies from all sides root for your success.

Follow these steps to gain allies:

Converse, don't compete: Seek to learn from others, not beat them in conversation. Don't try to top their stories or show off your knowledge. Refrain from petty arguments; if you disagree, raise your concerns diplomatically while dignifying opposing views.

Recognize what's right when you hear it: If you like what you hear, say so! At least nod or smile. Keeping a stone face won't endear you to speakers who may wonder if you're listening to them.

Satisfy WIIFM longings: Consider the self-interests of others when you're talking to them. Decide "What's In It For Me" from their point of view—and deliver the goods.

"Getting along with others is the essence of getting ahead, success being linked with cooperation."

—William Feather

11

Give Great Instructions

One of the biggest traps that managers fall into is they'll fail to communicate exactly what they want—and then they'll get mad when they don't get it.

Now that you're a manager, you'll find yourself giving instructions to employees throughout the day. What you say—and how you say it—will largely determine if they comply.

The task seems simple: Just explain what you want others to do and let them do it. But many obstacles can derail the process. Employees may not listen. You may not speak clearly. Even if they understand perfectly what you want, they may either refuse or otherwise fail to implement it.

You need to strike the right tone when giving instructions. If you overexplain or talk down to workers, they may resent your approach and feel demeaned. But if you bark a series of complex orders, they may wind up confused and unsure where to begin.

Problems can erupt if you rush your explanation or overdose on acronyms or other technical language. Your employees may not know as much about the situation as you do, so you may need to speak in simpler, more straightforward terms. Don't assume they will identify with your ways of thinking.

Customize your instructions to fit the personality and knowledge level of the employee. Consider the person's normal communication style, listening skills, and familiarity with the task at hand. If someone tends to skip ahead and miss key information, for example, you may want to number your steps and ensure the employee takes notes.

The risk increases when you instruct new employees, especially if they're just learning your business. Avoid jargon with new hires. Remove ambiguity from your statements. If any part of your instructions has multiple meanings, the odds of misinterpretation soar. That's when it's particularly crucial to specify how you intend for others to interpret or act on what you're saying.

Focus on action. If you preface your instructions with too much background, you can test listeners' patience. Inserting tangents or giving your opinion as you attempt to give directions will muddy your message. To ensure you deliver your instructions clearly, step into the employee's shoes and make sure you give an instant, one-sentence answer to the question, "What do you want me to do?"

For best results when you give instructions:

Rehearse: Organize your thoughts in advance. Practice on a friend. Confirm that you're able to instruct employees clearly and concisely.

Start simply: Move from the basic to the complex. Give employees a chance to ask questions along the way so they're confident with the fundamentals before having to absorb more complicated stuff.

Ask for a demo: Urge employees to demonstrate their understanding. Don't just ask if they understand; invite them to prove it to you.

"The five steps in teaching an employee new skills are preparation, explanation, showing, observation, and supervision."

—Harold Hook

12

Get Feedback

Almost all new managers experience bouts of insecurity. They inevitably wonder, "How am I doing? What does the boss think of me? Am I on track to move up—or have I leveled off?"

Few managers get the answers they're looking for.

Despite the popularity of so-called 360-degree feedback—where you receive input from your employees, peers, and boss—many managers still wonder how they're perceived. Formalized feedback programs might help you gauge your skills and competencies, but they rarely shed light on your personality traits or the subtle people skills that influence how others respond to you.

Part of the challenge of ascending into management is coping with a lack of feedback, especially from above. Your boss might drop hints (or criticisms) from time to time, but chances are you don't receive ongoing input on certain aspects of your behavior or job performance.

In the absence of feedback, you might grow increasingly uncertain about your abilities. *You* think you're doing a fine job, but without validation from higher-ups your confidence is tested.

You need not accept this sorry state of affairs and remain in the dark about your performance. Choose the right time and the appropriate manner in which to probe for clues. Don't wait for your next performance review in six months or one year, which in itself can prove a letdown. Some executives put off these appraisals or rush through them in a cursory fashion.

Put out feelers so that colleagues and bosses can comfortably report what they think of you. When you turn in work, confirm they received it and ask if it met their needs. After you give a presentation, ask audience members in private if they felt their time was well spent. Follow up after you propose an idea to check whether your coworkers and senior managers approve of it.

Fish for feedback using these methods:

Try indirect queries: If you're on good terms with someone, you can come right out and ask, "Can you give me your honest feedback?" But few people will respond with complete, forthright answers. It's sometimes better to give yourself feedback and see how they react. Example: "I see two areas I need to improve—listening and negotiating contracts. Would you agree?"

Establish a baseline: Once you get to know how someone talks, you can read between the lines when the person gives you feedback. When someone who prefers words such as "good" or "OK" calls your work "superb," such an uncharacteristically strong endorsement is revealing.

Depersonalize: Rather than ask point-blank for feedback, speak in general terms. Example: "What do you think of people who insist on turning in defect-free work even if it takes them longer?" That's better than saying, "Am I a perfectionist who does good but slow work?"

"Success is all about feedback, feedback, and feedback. You can't run mechanical systems without it, and you can't run organizations without it either."

—Barbara Reinhold

13

Speak with Power

As much as former secretary of state Alexander Haig craved power, he sure didn't talk like a blunt commander. He liked to use phrases such as "caveat my response" and "careful caution." Speaking like a bureaucrat not only undermines your point but also makes it harder for others to understand and trust you. Set a goal as a manager of becoming a plain-spoken, no-nonsense communicator.

Even if you ascended into management thanks to your technical know-how or your track record of hard work, a good bit of your success now rests on your ability to speak with power. When you talk, you need to ensure others listen.

A mumbling or wishy-washy speaker will prove a dud as a manager. You must state your position clearly and make it hard for others to ignore you. At the same time, you don't want to dominate every conversation.

Strong communication skills revolve around your voice tone, body language, and word choice. By speaking at an appropriate pitch, pace, and volume, you make it easier for people to understand you. By standing tall, gesturing naturally, and making friendly eye contact, you radiate poise and leadership. And by choosing vivid words to make your point and limiting your use of qualifiers, you add clarity and force to your remarks.

Powerful speakers home in on their main point. They chop away fluff and use the fewest words possible to express their core message.

If you see yourself as shy or soft-spoken, that's no excuse to waffle. Giving a halfhearted analysis of all sides or quietly muttering your approval or agreement will not impress your audience. Even if you're bashful or self-effacing, speak in bold, unambiguous terms. Don't drop subtle hints when the situation calls for you to speak up and be specific.

If you want to persuade others, realize that they're more likely to follow you if you're simple and direct. Don't waste words. Beware of giving too much information when trying to explain a point. Filter out extraneous data so that you talk about only what matters most.

Here are three ways to speak with power:

Emphasize action words: Before making an important point, identify the action word in your

sentence. Then pause for a half second or so just before and after you say it. Action drives meaning, so don't rush over your verbs.

Vary your volume: Powerful speakers are not monotone. They whisper to entice others to listen and raise their voice when they're excited or surprised. Keep tweaking the dial on your voice volume to reflect the ebb and flow of conversation.

Paint word pictures: Speak in visual terms to captivate listeners. Rather than tell them what to think, describe what you see in precise, colorful language.

"The finest eloquence is that which gets things done."

—David Lloyd George

14

Win Over Cynics

Ignore cynics at your own peril.

Left unchecked, cynics can drain an organization of its enthusiasm and commitment to excellence. They think they already have all the answers, so they don't listen to reason. Laughing off their sarcastic cracks isn't a long-term solution, because they'll perceive your meek response as a green light to intensify their antics.

One of your toughest tasks as a manager is to shut down cynics and prevent them from infecting morale. It requires constant vigilance.

When employees make caustic comments, challenge them to take a point of view and support it. Don't accept cynical asides if you privately agree or if you're relieved the jab isn't directed at *you*. Respond to all such commentary consistently.

Say that a clerk, Tom, lambastes the "suggestion box" program at your company. Don't nod or roll your eyes as he dismisses the program as a "joke."

Even if you share Tom's disdain for the program, don't say so. Instead, invite him to elaborate. Ask, "What specific steps do you think we can take to improve the program?" Shift the focus from griping to problem solving.

Some cynics need a safe outlet to vent their opinions and observations. You may want to assign a trusted employee to "buddy" with the cynic and serve as a sounding board. Have them meet periodically to share ideas and plan projects. Choose a "buddy" who can withstand cynicism well and who's skilled at redirecting sarcasm into positive action.

When you enable cynics to unleash their stinging jibes in private, they'll be less prone to disrupt staff meetings. Better yet, others will not follow a cynic's lead if they're not exposed to the troublemaker's scathing outbursts.

Rookie managers sometimes stamp someone as a cynic and then disregard that person's views. Ignoring cynics doesn't make them go away.

Also avoid labels. If you view Jim as "Mr. Sarcasm" and refer to him that way behind his back, he may find out, and his attitude might worsen. Nip cynicism in the bud by asking perpetrators to cut back on their biting commentary. Meet with them one-on-one and confront the issue head-on.

To tame cynics:

Remove obstacles so their jobs become easier: If they have a valid point, act on it. Fix a bottleneck in the system that addresses their grievance. Reward their constructive proposals with a quick response to prove that cynicism doesn't pay.

Let critics stage experiments: Empower cynics to take matters into their own hands—within reason. Allow them to make conditional changes as they see fit. Give them limited authority and track the results together. Let them exert power and they'll have less to complain about.

Demand evidence: Cynics tend to make harsh comments without offering support. By asking, "What facts do you have to support that?" you can expose the shaky foundation of their argument. And if they do present a cogent case, help them see how they can enact change by wooing allies rather than adopting an attack mode.

"When it comes to people and their quirks, idiosyncracies, and personality flaws, the variety seems to be limitless. The manager's aim remains the same: to keep these human beings from clogging up the workings of their group."

—Andrew S. Grove

15

Prepare for Change

Articulate a vision for your employees and you help them appreciate their role in contributing to the organization's success. That's especially important during times of change.

By defining a new direction to move forward, you reassure employees of the benefits of change. You shouldn't have to do this alone. Ideally, your senior management should already know why change will enhance the organization—and give you talking points, which you in turn should pass along to your staff. You can thus become a champion of change by spreading the gospel from above and endorsing it with your own brand of enthusiasm.

If you're left adrift to help your team weather change on its own, don't despair. Identify the advantages of change from your employees' point of view. Appeal to their self-interest and specify what's to gain in both the short- and long-term perspectives. If two offices are consolidating into one, for

instance, you might alert workers that this will result in better communication with their peers and bosses, better access to technology that makes their jobs easier, and cost savings to the company that will in turn improve their job security.

Beware of sloganeering. Skip the platitudes like "Change is a constant around here" or "We must change or die." Clichés ring hollow with employees. Instead, anticipate their questions and concerns—and be ready to answer them.

If a change may lead to layoffs, relocations, or other upheavals that directly affect employees, gather the facts in advance. You may want to develop and distribute a question-and-answer sheet so that employees can read for themselves what's going on and how it will alter their daily routine.

Spend lots of time in informal meetings with your team. The more you can chat face-to-face about the nature of the change and what it'll mean to employees, the more you can dispel rumors and gain their trust about what's in store. Make yourself accessible to everyone.

New managers may not be in the loop about what's going on, so level with workers if you don't have all the answers. Saying, "I don't know but I'll find out and get back to you" works better than barricading yourself in your office and becoming aloof.

Lay the groundwork for change by taking these steps:

Dangle rewards: Explain to the employees what goodies await those who are most adaptable to change. If they can secure a larger office, better equipment, or more flexible hours, they might treat change more openly and lower their resistance.

Anticipate multiple outcomes: Employees will want you to tell them the upshot of change: How will things be different? Answer by presenting a range of outcomes and specify what variables will determine how the change will develop.

Withhold negative opinions: Present change in a positive or at least neutral light to employees. Don't dwell on your displeasure with it—or they'll follow your lead and gripe even more.

"Employees don't resist change. They resist being changed."

—Peter Scholtes

16

Muzzle Your Mouth

The most dynamic communicators don't say much.

Instead of trying to talk louder and more force-fully than everyone else in the room, charismatic managers grab everyone's attention by treating their words as a precious resource. They speak only when they have something to say.

Silence enhances your power. By keeping quiet, listening well, and expressing your points in the fewest words possible, you gain a persuasive edge. Your employees will know that every word counts—and they'll give you their undivided attention as a result.

Plagued by nervousness and uncertainty, some new managers talk too much. They'll repeat simple instructions to the point where employees feel insulted. They'll tell long, rambling anecdotes that don't serve a clear purpose to advance the conver-sation. They will interrupt speakers and change the subject. Every time this happens, it threatens to

drive away employees who may think, "This person isn't interested in listening to me, so why should I listen to him or her?"

To muzzle your mouth, you need to appreciate the power of silence. That's easier said than done. Many people grow self-conscious during moments of silence in a conversation. Managers may worry that they appear unsure of themselves unless they always have something to say.

By keeping silent, managers often communicate loud and clear. A pregnant pause can convey approval, disapproval, concern, curiosity, or myriad other thoughts. It depends on the context of the conversation, your timing, and your facial expression.

Muzzling your mouth works especially well when you want to calm frayed nerves—your own or someone else's! Silence gives everyone a chance to reflect on the situation, rather than inflame it further by making emotionally charged comments.

Another danger of overtalking is that you can bore listeners. Restless employees may no longer heed your directives if you tend to babble. They may start daydreaming the minute you launch into your remarks, thus missing critical pieces of information that you want them to understand.

When you feel the urge to talk, ask yourself if it can wait. Purse your lips shut, breathe evenly, and listen.

To tap the power of silence:

Apply the 80/20 rule: In one-on-one conversations, try to listen for 80 percent of the time and limit your speaking to the remaining 20 percent. That requires asking questions to get others to open up.

Stop after you ask a question: When you pose a question, stop. Wait for an answer. If you do not get a prompt response, don't rush to answer your own question or skip it and raise another topic. Waiting in silence for 5 or 10 seconds may seem like an eternity, but it's sometimes the only way to learn what others think.

Let people vent: When someone is angry or agitated and needs to blow off steam, keep quiet. Saying, "Calm down" or "I understand" too often will only make matters worse. (The person may reply, "I *am* calm!" or "No, you *don't* understand!")

"Listen long enough and the person will generally come up with an adequate solution."
— Mary Kay Ash

17

Pose Penetrating Questions

One of the most overlooked success traits of managers is their ability to ask necessary questions of their employees. The act of asking in itself places you at risk. You may offend or annoy others with your tone or word choice. And you may not like the answer.

Yet questions are irreplaceable tools that enable you to learn. No manager can function well without asking employees lots of questions. By phrasing your inquiries wisely and watching your timing, you increase the odds that workers will level with you.

Employees who have worked for a less inquisitive supervisor may welcome your questions. They may appreciate your willingness to listen and learn, rather than simply tell them what to do. Through your questions, you can uncover ideas and opinions that workers had previously suppressed because no one else had shown interest.

Show interest in each answer. Express thanks when you're given a particularly informative response. Wait an extra few seconds after it appears the speaker's finished before you jump in. This allows others to add more revealing comments that they might otherwise keep to themselves.

Only ask questions if you're genuinely interested in the answer. Staffers can tell in an instant if you don't care about the response. Your distracted air, vacant stare, or flat voice tone may signal that you're going through the motions rather than making a concerted effort to learn. And don't reel off a series of rapid-fire questions or you may lapse into interrogation mode.

Watch your body language as you listen to the response. Remain still and attentive. If you're jittery or your eyes dart around the room, others may sense you're not interested in hearing their answers.

Refrain from excessive nodding and smiling. In your attempt to look supportive, you might go overboard. When you finally tire of sending affirmative signals, the speaker may wonder if you no longer agree or understand what's being said. Also, don't feel you must cluck your tongue or chime in with, "Go on" or "I can imagine" every few seconds, as this can disrupt the speaker's concentration.

Here are some tips to pose penetrating questions:

Keep it simple: Separate statements from questions. Don't lace your inquiries with your observations or opinions. Using the fewest words possible helps you stick to the core question without confusing the issue.

Launch one extra probe: To show you're listening and to confirm you understand the answer, get in the habit of following up when you're discussing an important subject. Use phrases such as, "Just to make sure I got that . . ." or "So what you're saying is . . . ?"

Dig below the surface: Guide employees to think more rigorously. Gently bore into them by asking, "What's the significance of that?" or "What do you conclude from that?"

"My greatest strength as a consultant is to be ignorant and ask a few questions."

—Peter Drucker

18

Lift Poor and Mediocre Performers

Set a high bar. If you accept poor or mediocre performance from your employees, you'll wind up with a bunch of lowly underachievers.

Rookie managers need to push for excellence. Demand the most from people and they'll strive to deliver. Tolerate a halfhearted effort and you send a message that your standards are easy to meet.

By transforming middling workers into high-performance stars, you'll impress your bosses and earn a reputation as a hard-charging, results-oriented leader. Your employees will also feel better about themselves once they see they're part of an elite team. The desire to excel will feed on itself, and your staffers will no longer settle for second-rate work.

Accept shoddy performance from others and it'll bring out the worst in you. Your results may start to

slip. Surround yourself with mediocrity and it becomes harder to give 100 percent. In professional sports, there are many examples of athletes who struggle while playing for a last-place team only to bounce back when they're traded to a play-off contender. The fact that they're suddenly surrounded by a coach and teammates who expect and demand superior performance causes them to dig within themselves and produce better results.

When you spot subpar performance, get involved. New managers may mistakenly spend most of their time with their top employees and avoid everyone else. Ignoring loafers or below-average workers allows them to burrow into your unit. They'll become increasingly difficult to dislodge if you leave them alone.

Chip away at their unacceptable performance by setting incremental goals and cheering their efforts to improve. Reinforce what they do right by praising them. If they lapse into mediocrity, intervene and remind them of your high expectations.

Some workers will resist your entreaties. The more you demand excellence, the more they'll gripe. Don't dignify their complaining by nodding or looking sympathetic. Instead, sever eye contact as soon as they bellyache. This teaches workers that in order to earn your full attention, they must cut the complaints and commit to improving their performance.

To propel poor and mediocre workers to greatness:

Champion their strengths even if they don't: Emphasize what workers do right. Talk up their assets and make them realize how much more they can contribute by harnessing their full potential.

Challenge them to improve in increments: You can't turn slugs into stars overnight. Set short-term goals that require slightly more effort and effectiveness. With each incremental gain, you lift workers onto a higher level.

Enlist peers as mentors: Put your most driven, talented performers alongside your also-rans. Weak employees often respond well when they're influenced by more successful, supportive coworkers.

> **"We found the most exciting environments, that treated people very well, are also tough as a nail. There is no bureaucratic mumbo jumbo . . . excellent companies provide two things simultaneously: tough environments and very supportive environments."**
>
> **—Tom Peters**

19

Criticize Without Criticism

As a new manager, there will be times that you'll need to criticize your employees. You'll dread it at first. But with practice it will become easier.

Dishing out criticism tests your communication skills. If you do it right, you can transform it from a negative, stinging message to an empowering, motivating experience for all involved.

Your tone and word choice drive your success. If you sound pained or exasperated, you're already in a hole. Employees will sense your irritation and cringe in despair. And if you're too abrupt, your criticism can come across as hurtful.

Choose words that fairly address the issue at hand. Avoid "always," "never," or "worst," which overstate the case and cause workers to respond defensively.

Also avoid the verbs "is," "was," "has," and "are." These words assign blame—and they equate a person with a faulty characteristic. Example: replace "Jack is lazy" with "Jack needs to make more calls

during the workday." Words work against you when they lead to generalizations or value judgments that grossly exaggerate a performance problem.

Yet words work for you when they describe observable behavior and paint visual pictures of the employee's actions. By saying what you see, your criticism is rooted in solid evidence. And you make it harder for the worker to argue or debate with you.

Before you criticize, ask yourself, "What is the person doing?" Make sure your answer captures exact behavior. If you resort to words such as "slow," "careless," or "unacceptable," you're not reporting actual events; instead, you're judging and labeling someone's behavior.

As a rule, give criticism in private. You don't want to make employees feel self-conscious. Also, begin on a positive note. Use phrases such as, "This may help . . ." or "Here's an idea . . ." And never criticize an employee's personality; limit your comment to specific actions you want the person to modify or improve.

Speak in a sincere, upbeat manner. If your criticism is well intentioned, there's no reason to sound hesitant, stern, or downbeat. Your enthusiastic tone will set the stage for the individual's response.

Do not criticize at the same time that you're unleashing pent-up frustration. Managers with fiery tempers should express criticism only when they're calm and in control.

Here's how to give constructive criticism:

Be direct: If you're uncomfortable, you might skirt the issue. But talking around it only prolongs the agony. State your criticism succinctly, free from babbling or dropping hints.

Check your assumptions: Make sure you have faith in the employee to improve. Criticize with the underlying belief that "you're capable of doing better," not "you're a lost cause."

Preserve the employee's self-esteem: Let your employee save face by saying, "Maybe you're not aware of this . . ." or "Here's one suggestion, and I'd like to hear your ideas."

"Never criticize until people are convinced of your unconditional confidence in their abilities."
—John Robinson

20

Beat the Clock

There's no mystery to managing your time. It takes discipline, concentration, and commitment.

New managers may attend time-management seminars and purchase elaborate "efficiency systems" (which usually consist of blank diaries, logbooks, and daily calendars) under the mistaken impression that they need to load up on fancy tools to succeed.

In fact, all you need is a strong dose of will.

Managing your time requires that you identify your sloppy work habits and fix them. By isolating the wasteful ways in which you plan and perform your job, you can find solutions that enable you to accomplish more in less time.

Rookie managers often struggle with time-management problems relating to procrastination. The new job overwhelms them, and they wind up juggling dozens of priorities at once. They start plenty of projects but rarely finish them.

To combat procrastination, investigate why you don't want to complete what you start. What's stopping you? Usually, the answer reveals your lack of confidence in the result, your uncertainty over what to do next, or your dislike of the nature of the work itself. To take a common example, new managers who are riddled with self-doubt may fear that by completing a task promptly and turning it in, they'll be vulnerable to criticism and thus prove they're ill-equipped to manage effectively. As a result, they play it safe and stall.

It's normal to worry that you'll be perceived as an impostor posing as a manager. Wave off the anxiety, bear down, and deliver the best work you possibly can. Adopting this attitude keeps you on track and enables you to manage your time more productively.

Realize that making a to-do list isn't a solution. It's merely a tool. The endless drafting and redrafting of lists can actually become an impediment that prevents you from taking action. If you're going to list your daily or weekly priorities, keep it simple, and assign a reasonable deadline for each item.

Don't confuse hectic activity with productivity. Immersing yourself in "busywork" might seem satisfying, but you may lose your perspective. Determine what's truly important and shift your attention where it's needed most.

To squeeze the most out of every workday:

Eliminate time wasters: Identify time killers such as aimless Internet surfing or long, chatty phone calls that divert you from more pressing duties. While it's fine to take short breaks, make sure you *earn* those breaks.

Set realistic standards: Poor time managers tend to be perfectionists. They may dread doing something imperfectly so they refuse to finish it. Strive for excellence, not perfection.

Stage "15-minute bursts": Set a timer for 15 minutes and plunge into a specific task. Even if you don't finish, you'll make headway and generate momentum.

"If you ask [people] what percentage of time they are spending on things that are urgent but not important, most would say 'Half the time.'"

—Stephen Covey

21

Impress Your Boss

Just as you manage your employees, you need to manage the boss. Your management career will take off if you can show higher-ups that you're a reliable, trustworthy star.

The very thought of trying to impress the boss may make you cringe. The notion of currying favor with powerful people at your organization may strike you as a fake, calculated attempt to get ahead.

There's a right and wrong way to impress VIPs. If you exceed expectations, anticipate and address a boss's concerns, and consistently look for ways to add value, you'll shine. But if you show off, bad-mouth colleagues, and hog credit for team accomplishments, you'll muddy your reputation and lose any chance of advancement.

Speak in can-do language. Bosses will heed your comments if you sound like you're organized, enthusiastic, and eager to deliver results. When they

ask you a question, give a one-sentence overview before you dive into the details. For example, start by saying, "We have three options" or "Let's examine this on three different levels."

Look ahead when discussing the status of a project. Focus on what will happen next rather than rehash what's already occurred. And never admit you're in wait-and-see mode. It's better to say, "We're going to make progress when we resume our meeting next week" than "I'm waiting for a return call so we can schedule a meeting next week."

When the boss asks you to do something, respond with confidence. Say, "I'll have that for you by 8:00 tomorrow morning" rather than "I'll try to get that to you tomorrow morning." Don't leave yourself an out. Executives grow suspect of managers who lace their remarks with qualifiers and back off from making bold commitments.

Look for patterns in your interaction with your superiors. Anticipate what issues or requests the boss will raise and be ready to answer. If you promise to do something, follow through promptly. Never make your boss nag you.

Most important, adopt a "no excuses" policy. Failing to produce results almost guarantees that a boss will doubt your abilities. When you're asked to give a progress report, start by summarizing what you've done, not what you haven't been able to do. Say, "Here's where we are" or "So far, we've

achieved these five goals." Don't say, "I haven't had a chance to . . ." or "I'm hoping that soon I can . . ."

Prepare to delight the boss by taking these steps:

Arm yourself with answers: Think in advance of what the boss will ask you—and prepare concise answers. Research the facts and gather the latest information so you're ready to impress with your vast knowledge of an issue.

Underpromise and overdeliver: Set time frames that you can beat. List your project objectives—and then accomplish all of them along with tossing in something extra. Consistently go beyond what's expected and you'll stand out.

Challenge in private: Wait for a calm moment to question a boss's order. Make sure no one else can overhear. Never object to the boss's comments in public.

"Managing one's superior is very similar to managing your own customers. In both situations, it simply involves managing human beings and relationships."

—Cynthia Loh

22

Mix and Mingle

Now that you're a manager, you'll need to upgrade your networking skills. Master the art of small talk and you can build alliances and develop key contacts both inside and outside your organization.

There's no secret to effective mingling. You simply need to approach strangers at mixers and industry conferences, introduce yourself, and ask a friendly question to get the conversation rolling.

Same goes if you're at a company-wide meeting and you don't know the folks sitting next to you. Turn to them and say, "Hi, my name is . . ." Mention where you work and let the dialogue flow from there.

If you look like you're going through the motions, people will notice. They will detect your lack of enthusiasm or your periodic sighing. Your flat voice tone will convey boredom. And if your eyes wander while someone's speaking to you, it'll appear as if you couldn't care less what they have to say.

Pretending to care when you're distracted or bored will backfire. It's better to muster the energy and curiosity to learn from each encounter, even if you're exhausted or preoccupied.

Think in advance of a few icebreaker questions you can ask. Examples include, "What did you think of the speech?" or "How long have you been participating in this group?" Solicit others' opinions without interrogating them, and they will open up to you.

Follow up on interesting points that speakers make. This proves you want to learn more from them. Don't recite a litany of questions without acknowledging or reacting to the answers.

Look for openings in the conversation to express genuine praise or admiration. If speakers mention accomplishments, such as earning a professional designation or getting a new office or new job title, congratulate them. Prolong their pleasure by asking more questions about their latest triumphs.

When mingling within your company, don't assume your colleagues in other departments (or even your bosses!) know what you're doing. They may not ask what you're working on and how it's going, so you should keep a running list of talking points to weave into the conversation.

To enhance your networking:

Keep it positive: When you meet a stranger, stick to safe, upbeat subjects. Don't complain or talk critically of others.

Restate before you respond: If you need time to mull over an answer or you're uncomfortable with the question, repeat in slightly different words what someone just said. This encourages him or her to elaborate, which in turn helps you buy time to plan the most diplomatic answer.

Know in advance who'll attend: Leave less to chance by reviewing the guest list. That way, you can identify influential people you want to meet and plan how you'll approach them.

"The suggestion to 'network' is nothing more than a fancy way of saying, 'Talk to people.'"

—Peter Vogt

PART 2
BEING AN EFFECTIVE LEADER

Should you care about developing your leadership skills? You should care. By developing your leadership skills, you are assured a more rewarding and successful career. You will make a greater difference in every organization in which you work. You will lift the performance of everyone who works with you. If you aspire to greater responsibility and the rewards that follow, then learning how to be a better leader is a necessary step to getting there. Opportunities and rewards in your organization will surely increase if you are an effective leader.

Your organization (whether a hospital, a government agency, a business, or a school) needs you to be a strong and effective leader. There is a high correlation between leadership effectiveness and the results that leaders produce. Developing an adequate cadre of leaders to perpetuate their organization is the number one preoccupation of CEOs in today's large corporations.

What's more, your organization needs you to be more than "adequate" in your leadership. While those who learn to lead get better results than those who don't, one startling conclusion presented in this book is the huge difference between the merely good and the extraordinary leader.

Unfortunately, the concept of leadership continues to be shrouded in misunderstanding. Ask 100 people to define leadership, and you are sure to get 100 different responses. So one objective of this book is to provide a simple and practical definition of leadership. It is not based on the subjective impressions of the authors but comes from solid empirical research.

Based on analysis of more than 20,000 leaders, there are 16 behaviors that differentiate the best leaders from the least effective. These are the behaviors that subordinates, peers, and bosses notice. These are the behaviors that you should work on developing.

Many leaders mistakenly believe that the path to greatness lies in finding their least effective traits or skills and then bringing those so-called "weaknesses" up into an acceptable range. These leaders believe that by removing these lower scores, they will be perceived as much more effective leaders.

Great leaders are defined by their having a small number of real strengths. Exceptional leaders don't become successful because they are flawless. And,

conversely, they are not exceptional leaders because they do 180 things remarkably well. These strengths can catapult leaders into the 90th percentile. Those people then make enormous contributions to the success of their organizations and their employees.

"Great leaders are not defined by the absence of weakness, but rather by the presence of clear strengths. The key to developing great leadership is to build strengths."

23
Leaders Can Be Made

When the subject turns to leadership, someone inevitably asks, "Isn't leadership something you either have or you don't? Aren't leaders born that way? Can people really become leaders?" These questions are as hardy as cockroaches—they just won't die.

In fact, leadership characteristics can be developed. You can be a better leader. It is true that some leadership characteristics show up very early in life, but it is also true that people often can't predict who will become the superstar leaders. Some people come into the world endowed with self-confidence and a keen intellect. That is clearly an advantage. But nearly all people are made better leaders from specific developmental activities. Leaders are a lot more "made" than they are "born."

Among the best evidence that leaders can be created starting with "regular" people is the remarkable track record of the U.S. Marines. Marine

recruits often come from troubled or abusive homes. They are frequently casual users of drugs or alcohol or have minor convictions. They often have not attended college. All the usual predictors of success are generally absent in this group of individuals. Yet many marine recruits are transformed into effective leaders after a two- to three-year period and go on to display remarkable leadership skills as their careers continue.

Leadership experts James Kouzes and Barry Posner wrote, "We would be intellectually dishonest if we did not say that some individuals clearly have a higher probability of succeeding at leadership than others. But this does not mean that ordinary managers cannot become extraordinary leaders." Leadership potential can be developed. With effort and practice, you can move beyond the skills you're born with to be an excellent leader.

To build your leadership skills:

Believe that ordinary managers can become extraordinary: Your mind-set can make the difference.

Commit to learning the concepts in this book: The more you know about what makes a leader extraordinary, the better your chances are of being phenomenal.

Try out the skills: Incorporate these ideas into action. Make yourself a better leader.

"The most dangerous leadership myth is that leaders are born—that there is a genetic factor to leadership. Myth asserts that people simply either have certain charismatic qualities or not. That's nonsense; in fact, the opposite is true. Leaders are made rather than born."

—Warren G. Bennis

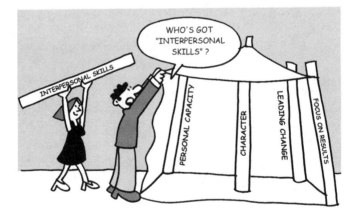

24

Raise the Leadership "Tent"

For decades, leadership experts have tried to find the list of distinctive traits that define great leaders. They assumed that each trait *stands alone*, much like the individually encased coil springs in an expensive mattress. As the advertisements demonstrate, if a bowling ball is dropped on one coil over here, the cup of water on the coil over there will not spill a drop. This metaphor suggests that leadership skills are solitary and independent, not intertwined, as we believe they are.

A more accurate metaphor for understanding leadership is a large tent, with the three-dimensional space under the canvas representing leadership effectiveness. *The poles in our metaphor represent key "strengths" of the individual leader*, especially those five that have been shown to make a difference in separating the great from the good: 1. *character*, 2. *personal capability*, 3. *focus on results*, 4. *interpersonal skills*, and 5. *leading orga-*

nizational change. The tent canvas represents all the possible competencies a leader might display.

The key to becoming a more effective leader is to lift more of the tent by hoisting multiple poles in the air. Lifting one tent pole pulls the entire tent up around that pole and raises a broad expanse of canvas. As a second competency pole is lifted, a new section of the tent is elevated, which not only raises the canvas above it but also raises the canvas between the two leadership poles. With each succeeding competency tent pole, large expanses of canvas are lifted, until ultimately there is a huge volume of space under the tent.

Some strategies for raising the leadership tent:

Develop critical competencies: Seek to be competent in each of the five leadership areas.

Develop a combination of competencies: The canvas will not be raised with just one or two competency poles in the air. Great leaders need a balance of complementary skills.

More is better: Leaders with strengths in each of the five areas will hoist the most impressive tents.

"Leadership behaviors are all knit together, much like the complex network of the human brain. There is an unbelievable interdependence between them."

—John H. Zenger and Joseph Folkman

25

Character Is the Essence of Leadership

The central tent pole in our leadership metaphor is *character*. Our research shows that a person who receives low marks on character has *absolutely no chance* of being perceived as a great leader, especially in the long run. Leaders who lack character must constantly be on guard that people will discover the truth about them. Like the Hollywood set that looks real from one side, they live in constant danger of having the illusion of their character dispelled if others see behind the facade.

What are the key elements of strong personal character? Leaders with character follow through on commitments. They keep their word. They make decisions with the good of the organization in mind, rather than a personal agenda. These leaders gain respect by being open and transparent. In fact, the more people can see inside, the more highly regarded the leader will be.

Leaders with character treat others with respect. They don't "smile up and kick down." The bellhop and the waitress get the same consideration as the CEO. Leaders with integrity look at others through a positive lens. They assume others have good intentions rather than bad. They look to collaborate rather than compete.

High-character leaders keep learning. They try new things and adjust rapidly to changing environments. They attempt to improve themselves constantly. They look for feedback and act on it.

Surely some must be wondering, "But can I *improve* my character? If so, how?" The answer might be surprising. Some believe the following chain of events is typical:

Character ⇨ Attitudes ⇨ Behavior

This sequence assumes you must first will your character into a new state; then your attitudes and behavior will follow. *But the fact is that people work very hard to make their attitudes, and ultimately their character, conform to their behavior.* If you successfully alter your behavior, there will be a remarkable transformation in attitudes and, eventually, character. In essence, we believe the following chain better maps reality:

Behavior ⇨ Attitudes ⇨ Character

We suggest the following steps to alter behaviors and ultimately character:

Always deliver: Be cautious in the commitments you make. Be careful not to overstate or over-promise what you can accomplish. Follow through. If you know you won't be able to keep a commitment, don't brush it under the rug. Admit it and reclarify your intentions.

Be humble: Be willing to laugh at yourself. Don't flaunt your authority. Humility will make you approachable. It opens the door to building relationships.

Find a mirror: You need to find out how others perceive your character. This mirror may be a good internal mentor, a trusted colleague or friend, or an effective 360-degree feedback process. Without this self-critical perspective, it is impossible to exert strong influence on a work group.

"Everything about great leadership radiates from character."

—Dave Ulrich

26

Develop
Personal Capability

The second critical tent pole of leadership is the *personal capabilities* the leader possesses. *These personal capabilities are not skills that would typically be described as leadership skills*, yet our research proves they must be in place for any individual to be perceived as a strong leader. Here are some of these individual capabilities:

- *Technical knowledge.* The best leaders have at least a working knowledge of the technological side of the business.
- *Product knowledge.* Great leaders need a thorough understanding of what the organization produces and why it is superior to competitive products.
- *Problem-analysis and problem-solving skills.* These skills include the ability to define problems, analyze them, and come up with solid recommendations for resolving complex issues.

- *Professional skills.* Excellent leaders must be able to write intelligently and concisely, make compelling presentations, organize their work efficiently, monitor progress, and work without close supervision.

- *Innovation.* This refers to a leader's ability to have a fresh outlook in approaching a problem, to shake loose from old methods, and to see new possibilities.

- *Initiative.* The best leaders see when something is falling through the cracks and immediately step in to make certain it is handled.

- *Effective use of information technology.* Great leaders set an example in the consistent use of e-mail, powerful software applications, and any technology that escalates performance.

Career experts Gene Dalton and Paul Thompson explain that the most successful leaders progress through a series of *four career stages that cannot be skipped*. Stage one is the time when individuals must prove they can learn the business and develop a solid foundation of technical expertise. In stage two, individuals continue to build technical skills and become *independent contributors*. By stage three, they become *mentors*—developing the careers and expertise of others. In stage four, they become *organizational visionaries*—leading the organization in new directions.

Too often, leaders reach a position they've been seeking and start to coast—believing that the learning phase of their career is over. They assume that there is a time for learning and a time for execution, and they are done learning. The best leaders *never* quit learning.

Here are some techniques to maximize your personal capability:

Understand the technology: Employees can see through attempts to cover up your lack of knowledge. Get up to speed by asking questions. Be willing to admit what you don't know.

Perfect professional skills: Managers can't manage unless they can communicate.

Try new things: Great managers innovate and take initiative. They think outside the box and don't hesitate to experiment.

"Leadership cannot be delegated to others."
—John H. Zenger and Joseph Folkman

27

Focus on Results

Leadership is ultimately about *producing results*. This is the third leadership tent pole. Leaders can have talent and character, but unless they produce sustained, impressive results for their organization, they simply are not good leaders.

One study of 1,000 managers showed that the best managers translate ideas into action. They push to take the next step forward by bringing energy, enthusiasm, and urgency to their role. They continually look for ways to improve. These leaders are in the driver's seat, with a foot on the accelerator—pressed to the floorboard most of the time.

How do leaders focus on results? Extraordinary leaders do the following:

- Establish stretch goals for their people.
- Take personal responsibility for the outcomes of the group.

- Provide ongoing feedback and coaching to their people.
- Set lofty targets for the group to achieve.
- Personally sponsor an initiative or action.
- Initiate new programs, projects, processes, client relationships, or technology.
- Focus on organization goals and ensure that they are translated into actions by their department.
- Operate with speed and intensity; accelerate the pace of the group.
- Champion the cause of the customer.
- Balance long-term and short-term objectives.

The best leaders get things accomplished, even under duress. They choose the right goals and follow through.

These are some ways to bring about results:

Know what the organization expects: Ask, "What does the organization expect from my department?" "From me personally?" The answers can be quite eye-opening.

Stay focused on long-term results: We've all seen executives who can make earnings soar—temporarily. Extraordinary leaders resist the urge to sacrifice long-term for short-term results. They keep the welfare of the organization ahead of their own personal agendas.

Take action: Extraordinary leaders wake up in the morning with a plan and put it into effect. They don't always wait for permission before moving ahead. Instead, they simply try new things.

"Leaders who aren't getting results aren't truly leading."
—Dave Ulrich, Jack Zenger, and Norm Smallwood

28

Cultivate Interpersonal Skills

The fourth essential tent pole of leadership is *interpersonal skills*. Along with the central tent pole representing character, it probably holds the most canvas. This leadership skill has become more important over time, especially since the demise of the "command and control" styles of leadership. Of all the competencies, interpersonal skills seem to make the most difference in whether leaders are considered extraordinary.

To develop strong interpersonal skills, leaders must do the following:

Communicate powerfully and prolifically. Extraordinary leaders don't hoard new insights. They tell people! These leaders give their work group a sense of direction and purpose. They help people understand how their work contributes to the goals of the organization. They err on the side of telling people too much.

Inspire others to high performance. Great leaders energize people to go the extra mile. They set stretch goals that motivate people to accomplish more than they think is possible.

Build trust. Superstar leaders act so that others trust them. They balance their concern for productivity and results with sensitivity to employees' needs and problems. When conflicts arise, they deal with employees' feelings as well as the technical aspects of the issue. They stay approachable.

Develop others. The most remarkable leaders support others' growth by giving honest and constructive feedback, balancing corrective with positive evaluations. They stay tuned to what is happening in employees' careers. They let others grow, even if it means letting them leave the department.

Collaborate and develop strong teams. Excellent leaders know not to insulate themselves from other team members and departments. They keep in touch, so that cooperative urges beat out competitive urges. They cultivate their team members' ability to work with diverse people.

Some key points for mastering people skills include:

Involve others in communication: One of the best ways to communicate is to get others to communicate! Interestingly, the worst communicators focus

solely on getting their message across. The best communicators check people's reactions and get their ideas.

Train everyone to be a leader: These days, leadership often gets passed around in a group. The person with the loftiest title and supposed power is no longer the one with all the answers. Believe that others are capable of great accomplishments and then watch them follow through.

To develop others, develop yourself: The best leaders create space for their employees to move up from below by raising their own performance. Their efforts not only set the example but also blaze a clear path for others to follow.

"If we treat people as they are, we make them worse, but if we treat them as they ought to be, we help them become what they are capable of becoming."
—Johann Wolfgang von Goethe

29

Lead Organizational Change

The *ability to lead organizational change* is the fifth tent pole of extraordinary leadership. The best leaders inspire people to rally around a change, while poor leaders have to push, cajole, or even threaten employees to accept change. A turbulent business environment puts leaders to the test: excellent leaders can turn a significant change into a pleasant journey, while poorly led change might be better described as a "trip through hell." With most organizations today in a constant state of change—from dramatic growth to downsizing and restructuring—leaders must be able to skillfully shepherd organizations in new strategic directions.

We're not talking about slight tactical shifts in current management processes or procedures. Caretaker managers can keep things going on a steady path. But if the organization is to rise to a significantly higher level of performance, extraordinary leaders must be able to sense the direction of the

market and alter the fundamental business model. They must be able to envision and create a new organization culture.

How do extraordinary leaders approach this task? The challenge in accomplishing change is not only to provide strong direction but also to get people involved in making the change work. The most effective leaders are able to strike a balance between directing change and involving others.

Leaders with strong directing tendencies are often prepared with well-organized plans that they communicate clearly. They maintain control, but they sometimes end up with employees feeling that changes are being done *to* them and not *with* them. The end result is that employees resist change and start to distrust management.

On the other hand, leaders who favor involving others in change sometimes fail to provide *enough* direction, leaving employees confused about their roles and what they need to do to keep the change moving forward. Sometimes leaders who tend toward involving others are simply unwilling to take risks or make tough decisions.

Our research shows clearly that both sets of behaviors are necessary for a leader to manage change effectively. Leaders need to help their people understand the specific details of the change and also help them feel involved so they will feel committed to the change.

Leading organizational change requires that you:

Create the overarching vision: Using your knowledge of the external environment, determine which trends to pursue and which to ignore. Stay involved in critical decisions. Use your influence to shape their outcome.

Translate the vision into specific objectives: In order to make the strategic vision happen, break it down to the level of specific tasks and expectations for individual workers. It is up to you to determine how resources will be allocated. You must establish the norms that will shape the culture.

Balance the need for direction with the need to involve others: Build support for your vision by getting people on board.

"Some people grin and bear it. Others smile and change it."

—Unknown

30

Find Your Leadership "Sweet Spot"

A psychologist once observed that the secret to life is discovering what "instrument" you are and then learning to play it. Woodwinds are no better than brass, nor are cellos superior to kettledrums. Each does something extremely well, and the musical score requires each unique contribution.

As individuals, we all have competencies and abilities that come to us more easily than others. We are drawn to some tasks and resist others. It is not difficult to see that, in any group of leaders, there are marked individual differences. One key to extraordinary leadership is finding the intersection of what you do well, what you love doing, and what the organization values.

One of our colleagues, Kurt Sandholtz, wanted to learn what causes people to have a "career best" experience—a time when they felt they were making a significant contribution and were very successful. After asking thousands of people, "What is

the best job you've ever had?" he found that "career bests" have three common characteristics:

1. "Career bests" tap into a person's talents or competencies. When people are performing their best, they are almost always using skills, knowledge, or expertise that sets them apart from others.

2. A "career best" experience builds on what people are passionate about. Passions are things we love to do, regardless of how well we do them. For example, some love to sing in the shower, despite knowing they do not do it well.

3. "Career bests" inevitably add value to the organization. When people describe their ultimate career experiences, they don't say, "I was very competent and loved doing this job, but no one in the organization noticed."

When you find the area of intersection of your competencies, your passion, and organizational needs, you will find that you feel more engaged and motivated and that work is just more fun. In addition, you will be adding more value than your colleagues—and your performance ratings will reflect that.

To find your personal leadership "sweet spot":

Determine your strengths and passions: Ask yourself these questions: What do I do extremely well? When people talk about my abilities, what do they

mention first? What activities energize me and bring me a great deal of personal satisfaction?

Determine what your organization values: Just as personalities are unique, so too are organizations. Look for what your organization needs. If it doesn't fit with what you enjoy and do well, look for an organization that *does* need what you have to offer.

Find the area of intersection: Extraordinary leaders find the spot where their competencies and passion overlap with an organizational need. This creates an opportunity for them to be and do their best.

"We are not in a position in which we have nothing to work with. We already have capacities, talents, direction, missions, callings."
—Abraham Maslow

31

Focus on
Building Strengths

Let's imagine that you have a renewed determination to improve your leadership effectiveness. To start the process, you participate in a 360-degree assessment of your competencies. In our experience, when people get feedback on their behavior, they always seem compelled to focus their attention on the items with the lowest scores. Something in our culture drives us to completely ignore our higher scores and shine a spotlight on the lowest ones.

Most people believe that fixing weaknesses will have a more powerful impact on leadership effectiveness ratings than building strengths. Where does this belief come from? Perhaps we learned it in school. After all, our teachers spent a lot more time correcting mistakes than focusing on what we did well. Or perhaps we feel compelled to be "Renaissance people," with remarkable talent in every area. Perhaps our performance appraisal process of

focusing primarily on deficiencies rather than strengths is to blame.

Ultimately, however, this strategy is not the most helpful for getting leaders from good to great. *What is much more effective in the long run is to focus on building strengths.* Peter Drucker once wrote: "Most problems cannot be solved. Most problems can only be survived. And one survives problems by making them irrelevant because of success. . . . One focuses on success, especially on unexpected success, and runs with it."

Here are some strategies for staying focused on strengths rather than weaknesses:

Understand that weaknesses sometimes deserve to be ignored: We can't all be Mary Poppins, famous for being "practically perfect in every way." If you've never been good at math, it's unlikely you'll be an engineer any time soon.

Improve what you do well: You will get more mileage out of focusing on your areas of expertise and skill. Make them even better!

Look for the strengths in others: If you want to get your employees from good to great, try encouraging them in their areas of talent.

"Do not think of your faults: look for what is good and strong and try to imitate it. Your faults will drop off like dead leaves, when the time comes."

—John Ruskin

32

Concentrate on Developing Three to Five Strengths

Imagine receiving the results of a 360-degree assessment that show your ratings as slightly above average on all competencies. You may feel relatively pleased. But you might not be so pleased if your child came home from school with all C+'s on his or her report card. Our research shows that just a few strengths can have a dramatic positive effect on the perception of a leader's effectiveness—but only when a competency stands out.

We wanted to understand how strengths affect overall leadership effectiveness, so we asked people, "What would you guess the overall effectiveness percentile would be for people with no strengths?" Most people indicated they thought a leader with no noteworthy strengths would be rated on average at the 50th percentile. However, our study of 8,000 leaders shows these leaders actually received ratings at the 34th percentile. *In other words, possessing no*

strengths plunges you to the bottom third in terms of perceived overall leadership effectiveness.

Why are leaders with no area of strength perceived to be in the bottom third? It's because they lack a redeeming quality, skill, or ability. They may not be *ineffective* at anything, but they also are not terribly *effective* at anything. Leaders with just one strength move from the 34th percentile to the 64th percentile, on average. *Imagine, a 30 percent increase just for possessing one strength!* This shows the powerful influence of being good at any one competency.

Our research shows that leaders with three strengths are rated at the 81st percentile, while leaders with five strengths rank in the top 10 percent— at the 91st percentile. When we have challenged leaders to move from the 50th percentile to the 90th percentile, their response was most often that it seemed impossible. Their perception was that they would need to be perfect in almost every competency to achieve such a high rating. That clearly is not so. We found that *to be at the 90th percentile simply requires a leader to be highly skilled at five competencies!* This seems achievable to most aspiring leaders.

To improve in a manageable number of areas:

Push yourself to improve: Possessing even one strength causes performance ratings to improve drastically.

Don't overextend: There are limits to what you can accomplish. Don't try to change everything at once. We suggest you focus on improving in no more than three areas at a time.

Focus on getting to great: Becoming an extraordinary leader is not impossible. The first step is knowing where to concentrate your energies.

"People can be successful at change only if they focus their effort in a few areas. We recommend a maximum of three areas of improvement at any one time."

—John H. Zenger and Joseph Folkman

33

Let the Halo Effect Work for You

One of our most interesting findings was that *some leaders seemed to be able to do no wrong*. These remarkable leaders tended to be rated at the 90th percentile on almost all competencies. Simultaneously, *some leaders could do no right*. Their ratings fell in the lowest percentile on almost all competencies. We believe that both sets of ratings are a distortion.

When leaders perform extraordinarily well on a few behaviors, people's impressions of them on other competencies tend to be distorted positively. The opposite effect seems to occur for those with a few profound weaknesses. The halo effect can be a useful tool for those seeking to improve their leadership skills.

We have all seen the halo effect in action. How many times have we been disappointed to hear a speech by a famous actor or athlete? Why did we believe that he or she would have something

insightful or even interesting to say? Just because a person can act or play sports does not mean he or she will have wisdom to share on other topics. We see the effect on the negative side when we demonize people who have made serious mistakes.

One explanation for the halo effect comes from fascinating research by Leon Festinger. Festinger describes how people experience tension when they believe two contradictory ideas, such as "My manager is a terrible leader" and "My manager is very good at solving complex and difficult problems." Hundreds of experiments have shown that people will do whatever is necessary to reduce the dissonance between conflicting ideas. When leaders improve their abilities in a few competencies, this creates a potentially useful dissonance in the minds of others. People ask themselves, "How can this leader be so effective on some things but less effective on others?" People then close the gap on the dissonance by shifting their beliefs. They assume leaders are more competent than they truly are, creating a positive effect for leaders who develop extraordinary strengths.

To take advantage of this halo effect:

Build up a few profound strengths: Not only will your strengths help produce positive results, but they will also create a powerful impression of competence.

Be great at what your organization cares about: You will get the most mileage from your strengths if they're in areas that are highly valued. If your organization cares most about excellent communication skills, make sure you communicate clearly!

Let people know your talents: While you don't want to alienate people by showing off, you do want to let people know your capabilities. The more they know your strengths, the more pressure they will feel to assume you have strengths in other areas too.

"If people have the general impression that a person is an extraordinary leader, they will overestimate this person's skills and abilities. The key is to get the attribution process to work for you rather than against you."
—John H. Zenger and Joseph Folkman

34

Fix Fatal Flaws

Magnifying strengths to the fullest has been one of the main messages so far. In the process, we may have implied that weaknesses should never be the focus of a personal development plan. However, in many cases, focusing on weaknesses is absolutely what needs to be done.

As we have already observed, people challenged to improve their leadership effectiveness have an amazingly similar plan for improvement.

1. Assess areas of strength and weakness. Since being really good or even moderately good at something means you don't have to worry about it, immediately scrutinize your low scores.
2. Decide which weakness is most significant, usually because it has the lowest score.
3. Develop a plan of action to address the weakness.

In fact, in some cases, working on a weakness *is* the best approach to improving. If a fatal flaw is not corrected, it will act as a drag on the overall perception of leadership effectiveness. We believe that even one extremely low score will produce a negative halo effect.

Frederick was the director of research for an international pharmaceutical company. A brilliant chemist, he towered over others in his grasp of the technical aspects of the research process. But his personal manner was curt and abrupt. He cut people off in meetings. He rejected suggestions or ideas for procedures that were not his own. The other department heads felt that he failed to listen to their input. After extensive feedback, Frederick began to change the way he treated others. Making changes in this one specific arena caused his overall ratings to escalate. Conclusion: if you have a fatal flaw, fix it.

An analysis of our data reveals five patterns of behavior that consistently lead to a failure in leadership. Possessing one or more of these virtually makes it impossible for a person to be perceived as an effective leader:

1. Inability to learn from mistakes
2. Lack of relationship-building skills
3. Lack of openness to new ideas
4. Lack of accountability
5. Lack of initiative

Lessons 36–40 will examine each of these fatal flaws and what must be done to fix them.

To combat fatal flaws:

Reflect on your experience: What have you learned from past events? Specifically, what did you learn from things that did not go well? What would you have done differently? What will prevent the same thing from happening again?

Assess whether you have any fatal flaws: Get feedback. Participate in a developmental survey to get a good overview of any weaknesses. Are any of your low scores on our list?

Make a specific plan: After reading lessons 36–40, you will have a better idea of exactly how to remedy fatal flaws.

"The real fault is to have faults and not try to mend them."

—Confucius

35

Look for Powerful Combinations of Competencies

Brett Savage, a longtime colleague, told the secret of his success playing high-school football. Brett had two attributes on his side. One was his height of 6 feet 4 inches, more the physique of a basketball player than a football player. The second was his ability to catch anything thrown anywhere close to him. Every time Brett went out for a pass, all the quarterback had to do was throw the ball just a little over Brett's head and the defensive backs were helpless to prevent him from catching it. As Brett explained, "The combination of height and good hands was powerful."

We were interested to see the impact of combinations of competencies on leadership ratings. To research this, we examined leaders who had been rated in the top 25 percent for interpersonal skills but were rated below the top quartile for focus on results. When we examined this group, we found that only 9 percent of these people were also rated as

excellent leaders. Clearly, interpersonal skills alone do not guarantee a high ranking on leadership.

When we examined those leaders who were ranked high in *both* interpersonal skills and focus on results, this group was *much more likely to be ranked as excellent leaders*. With both areas of expertise, these individuals now had a 66 percent chance of being ranked as excellent leaders! Both skills are valuable and lead to success, but the *combination* of being excellent at both skills together substantially increased the probability of overall effectiveness.

The secret to building success as a leader is to be excellent at powerful combinations of skills. We have found that there are many such powerful combinations. Some of the most useful combinations include personal skills in getting the work done coupled with the ability to encourage others to perform their work. The effect of powerful combinations is to erect and lengthen the tent poles that lift the overall leadership tent to new heights.

Here are some examples of these combinations:

- Technical knowledge and the ability to inspire or motivate others.
- Connecting with the outside world and the ability to inspire and motivate others.
- Focus on results and the ability to communicate powerfully and prolifically.

- Teamwork/collaboration and establishing stretch goals.
- Strategic perspective and problem-solving/analytical skills.

Some helpful methods for building combinations of competencies include:

Build complementary skills: Look for ways to improve on skills that work together to produce a whole greater than the sum of the parts.

Do some research: You can contact the authors at www.expgi.com to learn how to find out more about these powerful combinations. Determine which areas of improvement will best serve you.

Cross train: Sometimes the best way to strengthen one competency is to focus on another. You may want to first tackle skills that you are more likely to improve easily.

"Powerful combinations produce exponential results."

—John H. Zenger and Joseph Folkman

36

Learn from Mistakes

Some leaders show such promise that they are expected to go all the way to the top of their organizations—but then something happens to make them fall off the track. These "derailed executives" have been the subject of some fascinating research.

Morgan W. McCall, Jr., and Michael Lombardo found that derailed executives make about the same number of mistakes as those whose careers continue onward and upward, but derailed executives *do not use setbacks or failure in an assignment as a learning experience.* They hide their mistakes from others. They do not take immediate steps to rectify what they have done. And they tend to brood about the mistake, constantly reliving it for years afterward.

Those whose careers continue to soar do exactly the opposite. They readily acknowledge what happened, alert colleagues to the potential consequences, do their best to fix it, and then proceed to

forget about it and move on in their career. Our research confirms that *the inability to learn from mistakes is the single biggest cause of failure for leaders*. This is the first fatal flaw.

We can only speculate about the reasons for this. Is failure to learn from mistakes a symptom of not being willing or able to face reality, because it is painful? Does it show that people are unwilling to accept the fact that they could have done something wrong? Or do people genuinely not recognize the serious consequences of what they have done, believing instead, "That problem I had was no big deal. It doesn't really matter"? Perhaps people have never learned the skill of objectively analyzing their own behavior.

A CEO with a brilliant mind and many accomplishments had one fatal flaw. He made hasty decisions about whether to promote people, dismissing some as being incompetent after a 20-minute interview and promoting others because of one thing they had done or said. Despite countless warnings, the CEO selected as his VP of finance an executive with a terrible reputation for backstabbing and sinister political behavior. Eventually, the VP was successful in ousting the CEO, through an end run to the board. Several people commented, "We tried to tell him, but he would not listen." This CEO failed to change course, even after his mistakes were staring him in the face.

To best learn from mistakes:

Review past actions without cringing: Look back and examine what's happened. Where could improvements be made? Recognize that mistakes are part of the learning process. They can be valuable learning tools if you use them that way.

Tell others when you make mistakes: Hiding mistakes only makes their outcome worse. Share your pain, and the problem can begin to be solved. Be sure to inform those who will be affected by the mistake!

Solve the problem: Seek good advice from others you trust. Make adjustments. Then don't relive the past. Once you fix your mistake, move on.

"The team that makes the most mistakes wins."
—John Wooden

37

Build
Positive Relationships

One of the authors was having dinner with a friend who is currently a university president. When asked about what kinds of activities filled his day, he commented, "Well, today I had to fire a professor." Someone at the table asked, "Why? Was he incompetent?" "No," replied the president, "he was very current in his field! The problem was that no one in his department could remember a staff meeting that he attended that did not end in an argument. He was absolutely impossible to get along with and created so much friction in the department that nothing was getting done." In this case, the professor's lack of interpersonal skills made his other skills irrelevant.

This story highlights the second fatal flaw, which is the inability to build positive relationships. This flaw springs from two major sources: what we do wrong (errors of commission) and what we fail to do right (errors of omission).

Errors of commission. When leaders are abrasive, insensitive, browbeating, cold, arrogant, and bullying, this is a pattern that surely leads to failure in today's world. That behavior was tolerated 50 years ago but seldom is today. No combination of intelligence, hard work, business acumen, and administrative skills can compensate for this interpersonal ineptness. In the human resources profession, the saying goes: "We hire people for their technical competence and fire them for their interpersonal incompetence."

Errors of omission. We are often stunned to see the number of people in middle-management positions in organizations who do not follow some of the most rudimentary social rules:

- When you talk to people, look them in the eye.
- Learn and use people's names.
- When talking with people, say or do things that let the other person know you are listening and understanding.
- Do not dominate the conversation and take all the "airtime."
- Sincerely inquire about others' ideas and activities.
- Laugh at others' jokes and attempts at humor.
- Praise others' hard work and efforts in furthering a good cause.
- Smile when meeting and greeting other people.

Ways to build productive relationships:

Ask for feedback: It is the golden path to continual improvement. Accept feedback as the valid perceptions of others and seek to understand the meaning. Assume that the givers have pure, positive intent. Resist the impulse to retaliate.

Enroll in developmental experiences: The key is to move outside your comfort zone and do something that will provide real development. Invest in yourself. Take the necessary time off the job to attend.

Practice, practice, practice: Pick one skill to improve upon at a time. Keep a pocketful of pennies. Try to practice that skill 10 times a day. To help keep track, every time you use that skill, shift a penny from one pocket to the other.

"Being interpersonally inept inevitably sinks leaders."

—John H. Zenger and Joseph Folkman

38

Be Open to New Ideas

Leaders are often beset by twin demons—arrogance and complacency. Arrogant leaders believe their ideas are superior to everyone else's. Complacent leaders are simply unwilling to listen to others' ideas and experiment with them. They are content with the status quo.

Perhaps these leaders feel threatened by good ideas coming from others. Maybe they lack the energy to make changes. Maybe they grew up with the mistaken notion that those with the formal title of "manager" should have the answers to all problems.

This lack of openness to new or different ideas is the third fatal flaw. It can be a major turnoff to subordinates. Insisting on doing things the same old way can have two major negative consequences.

1. **Impact on subordinates:** People feel ignored, their ideas are unappreciated, and their contri-

bution undervalued. Under such leaders, morale degenerates and turnover escalates.

2. **Impact on the organization:** Good ideas and solutions fail to get implemented. Because good ideas are squelched, people stop thinking about better ways to do things. The organization stagnates.

Many consulting firms have developed a successful practice by interviewing employees and seeking their opinions and recommendations about the serious issues the organization faces. The consulting firm then presents these ideas to upper management, along with a hefty bill. The fact is, the employees would have been willing to tell the executives exactly the same things, had the executives asked. Many employees have told us that they and their coworkers have usually tried to pass on those messages, but no one was listening. The great ideas are there—if leaders will seek them out.

One senior executive shared his techniques for dealing with people who come to him with new ideas. He said, "I don't ever discourage a new idea. Ideas are tender and need to be nourished. So I ask lots of questions and give the person encouragement to pursue it, unless I'm positive it won't work. If I have the slightest belief it could succeed, I am enthusiastic about it. Over the years, that's paid off in some remarkable advancements."

Here are some ways to cultivate a climate that welcomes new ideas:

Ask people for their thoughts: Your best resources are all around you. Ask the people closest to the work for their ideas about how to do things better.

Shower ideas with enthusiasm: Give people an opportunity to think out loud. Ask them for details. Even if you can't implement an outrageous idea, sometimes the process will lead to a better alternative.

Infuse energy into the process: Let people know you will not let their ideas drop. Leaders need to capture and amplify the enthusiasm of others.

"Many of us have worked for leaders whose automatic response to every idea or suggestion was negative. It is impossible to calculate the damage such a person does inside an organization."
—John H. Zenger and Joseph Folkman

39

Be Accountable

Some managers seem to subscribe to the philosophy, "It doesn't matter if you win or lose, it's how you place the blame." These managers have fallen prey to the fourth fatal flaw—lack of accountability. Leaders who do not assume complete responsibility for the performance of a work group are bound to fail.

The accountable leader, on the other hand, identifies so strongly with the group that *the success of the work group equals personal success*. The responsible leader puts organizational goals ahead of personal ambitions and puts the welfare of the total organization ahead of his or her own department. The responsible leader does things for which there may be no immediate reward, but does them because they are the right thing to do and will help the organization in the long run.

Leaders must be accountable in their dealings with various groups:

Behavior with subordinates: Responsible leaders take complete charge of the group, never shirking decisions by wishing to remain "one of the group." They insist that individuals live up to their responsibilities. They are willing to terminate poor performers when necessary, understanding that the performance of the group is more important than salving the feelings of one person. Responsible leaders don't hesitate to take blame for failures but never fail to pass along credit for high-quality work. They invite subordinates to make presentations on the team's success to senior executives, to give them exposure and experience.

Behavior with upper management: Accountable leaders accept criticism for mistakes. They buffer their group from excessive criticism. They tenaciously ensure that the group meets the expectations of upper management. In circumstances where the work group is being held up by management indecision, the responsible leader must sometimes take a risk and press the executives to make timely choices.

Behavior with other groups: Responsible leaders do not let anything fall in the cracks between their group and other departments, suppliers, or customers. Instead of shrugging their shoulders and saying, "It is not my responsibility," accountable leaders say, "If it is not someone else's clear responsibility, then we'll do it."

Taking responsibility means being willing to do the following:

Shift your mind-set: Think in new ways about your responsibilities. Keep the big picture in mind. Visualize ways to get the organization where it needs to be.

Take the heat: You don't need to take responsibility for every bad event, but honestly evaluate what you could have done to prevent any failures. At the same time, heartily sing your workers' praises. Never miss an opportunity to tell others of the good work being done by the people around you.

Remember you're the boss: Sometimes it's up to you to do the unpopular thing. You may need to fire unproductive workers or push people to do better work. It's more important to be effective than liked.

"Management has no power. Management has only responsibility."

—Peter F. Drucker

40

Take Initiative

The fifth fatal flaw is the failure to make things happen. Aspiring leaders who lack initiative drive a huge nail into their own career coffins. Leaders must create results. They must be on the forefront of creating needed change.

One measure of a leader's effectiveness is the number of initiatives he or she personally champions. What projects has this leader started? What outcomes have this leader's fingerprints all over them? What has happened that would not have occurred had this leader not been present?

The leader with initiative stops to consider the current reality and asks questions such as these:

- What is missing that would make a big difference?
- What needs to be done that only I can do?
- What could I do that would make a significant difference to the performance of this work team?

If I had to pick one action step, what would it be?

■ What are others expecting me to do?

This leader then steps in and makes those things happen. This is a totally different approach from the leader who waits and responds to events after they happen. Action-oriented leaders must act like surfers. They need to be positioned in front of the wave to get a thrilling ride. Surfers who are a second too slow simply bob up and down in the ocean waiting for the next wave. Out in front is where extraordinary leaders must be.

We recommend that leaders take the initiative to implement a change in their organizations. The change could be as simple as implementing a new reporting system or as complicated as a new organizational structure. As Machiavelli noted, "There is nothing more difficult to carry out, nor more doubtful of success, nor more dangerous to manage, than to initiate a new order of things." But nothing builds leadership skills so effectively as the process of initiating change.

Taking initiative requires the following steps:

Study the organizational landscape: What changes are needed? Where should the organization be? Think several steps ahead.

Make an action plan: Determine what outcomes you plan to achieve and how you plan to achieve

them. After implementing the change, evaluate how well the change succeeded. What would work better next time?

Don't wait for more responsibility—take it: In one of the best studies of powerful developmental experiences, Anna Valerio concluded that nothing has more impact on a leader's development than being given a broader scope in his or her current assignment. Broader responsibility can be granted, or it can be self-generated. Try applying for a new technology transfer, implementing a new procedure, or volunteering to do more.

"You can't build a reputation on what you are going to do."

—Henry Ford

41

Learn from Feedback

Inside people's heads is a picture of how they see themselves. This mental self-portrait sums up their values, behaviors, and self-image. In most cases, leaders with a fatal flaw are totally unaware of that flaw. For example, people who immediately reject others' ideas would probably describe themselves as having such extensive experience that they know what ideas will succeed and fail. These individuals don't know they are perceived as rejecting everyone else's ideas. How can that be changed?

Feedback from coaching, team discussions, or 360-degree surveys can provide "disconfirming information." The messages conveyed would be contrary to leaders' self-perceptions. This creates a dilemma and forces action. Leaders now have several choices:

First, deny the information. But if it comes from multiple sources that are clearly reliable, it

becomes extremely difficult to deny this consistent pattern of feedback.

Second, choose to change their self-concept. Leaders can say to themselves, "OK, I guess I am arrogant and think my ideas are the only good ones that exist." However most would find this unacceptable and illogical.

Third, change behavior. For most people faced with a barrage of disconfirming information, the easiest course of action is actually to change the behavior. That is the power of feedback.

Not all feedback is equally useful. Feedback is most valuable if it is specific, focused, and related to the behavior or process rather than general personality characteristics. The most useful feedback focuses on the intensity of effort, the innovative approaches used, or the ability to overcome obstacles. If a child is told, "Wow, you really worked hard on that," he or she will be better equipped to face future challenges than if told, "Wow, you're really smart." This is a subtle difference in the way feedback is given, but it can powerfully affect the way people view themselves and their abilities.

Not all people like the same type of feedback. Some people are highly motivated by positive feedback. They feel crushed by negative feedback. However, other people are skeptical of positive feedback because they care most about averting failure. To

them, negative feedback is a source of useful information, while positive feedback comes across as hollow praise.

The fine art of learning from feedback will be easier if you do the following:

Find trustworthy sources of feedback: It's easy to get blindsided by our own weaknesses. We need people we can trust who will tell us the truth about ourselves. Don't shy away from giving good feedback to others.

Stick with specifics: Excellent feedback gives people specific information. Give detailed examples where possible. Describe what actually happened rather than your assumptions about the events.

Tailor feedback to the person: Be sensitive. If the person's life orientation is to prevent disaster, stick with suggestions for improvement to help him or her achieve that goal. If individuals will be devastated by negative feedback, accentuate the positive aspects of their performance.

"Not to know is bad; not to wish to know is worse."

—African proverb

42

Take a
Nonlinear Approach

Warfare through the 1700s to the middle of the 19th century was characterized by two groups of soldiers marching in rows straight toward each other. Not until the American Revolution did soldiers begin hiding behind trees and lying on the ground to avoid being easy targets. This was an entirely different type of war. We propose a similarly radical approach to developing leadership skills.

If you were to decide to improve a leadership skill, such as your level of technical expertise, you might examine your current performance and determine a list of actions, such as:

1. Sign up for a class.
2. Attend professional workshops.
3. Read technical/professional journals.
4. Read the latest books in the technical/professional field.
5. Broaden your network; ask for coaching or mentoring on specific topics.

This tactic is a classic, linear, frontal assault. This plan plots a straight line from where you are to where you want to be. It is extremely logical and characteristic of many people's propensity to identify a challenge, put their heads down, and run straight at it full force. Our claim is that linear plans work best for people moving from poor performance to good performance. However, moving people from good to great is best accomplished with a nonlinear approach.

Let's examine what a nonlinear path might look like. As we have mentioned previously, certain leadership skills are linked together as what we call "competency companions." *We propose that the best way to make improvements in one skill is sometimes to make improvements in the competency companion skill, not the targeted skill itself.*

For example, if you wanted to develop greater technical competence, you could focus directly on improving that skill, but you might have more success with improving your technical competence if you focus on its "competency companion," which is interpersonal skills. Robert Kelly found evidence for the usefulness of this nonlinear approach in his research on the most productive scientists at Bell Labs. The most competent scientists did not end up being those with the highest IQ or most knowledge. They were the ones who used interpersonal skills to get their work done. They helped colleagues,

showed concern, asked others for ideas, and gave others credit.

To benefit from a nonlinear approach:

Change your mind-set: The best way to improve in one area may be to ignore it! Instead, you may do better to focus on a related area of improvement.

Build your awareness of competency companions: You will need to know which skills are interrelated in people's minds as characteristics of effective leaders. To find out more about the *Competency Companion Development Guide* by Zenger and Folkman, contact the authors at info@expgi.com.

Savor the side effects: Developing competency companions can change a person. Just as learning to play golf gives you increased confidence, so strengthening a competency can change your perspective and outlook on life, making you more effective in many areas.

"There is no such thing as working on only one leadership quality or attribute. When you improve one, you will invariably be improving several others."
—John H. Zenger and Joseph Folkman

43

Take Steps to Improve Leadership Skills

Every aspiring leader can take steps to improve. One of the best places to start is to understand what you do well and capitalize on it. Peter Drucker argued, "Self-development is *making oneself better at what one is already good at*. It also means *not worrying about the things one cannot be good at*." To do this, Drucker advised taking an inventory of major accomplishments in the recent past.

- List your major contributions to the organization over the past two or three years.
- Specify precisely the things the organization expects from you.
- Be clear about what you cannot do as well as what you can do.

By listing past successes, you will have a better understanding of where you are likely to make significant contributions in the future. Think back to high school and college. Let's assume you were

extremely adept at mathematics but you did not enjoy language study much nor did you do well at it. Which path should you choose going forward? Do you work hard at becoming better at language? Or do you decide to leverage your talents in mathematics and excel in that area?

We believe it makes sense for you to lead with your areas of strength. No one can do everything. You will feel more motivation, make more progress, and experience more success if you focus on areas that you like and in which you do well. Sometimes the best strategy is to play to your strengths and find ways for others to fill in the gaps. Through delegation, the use of outside resources, or reallocation of work assignments, you can find ways to make your weaknesses irrelevant.

Another excellent strategy for becoming an extraordinary leader is to observe expert leaders around you. Watch how they handle tough situations, particularly when they do it right. Many organizations are not leaving this process to chance these days. They are hiring professional coaches to give objective, constructive feedback to senior leaders. The higher people move in the organization, the less apt they are to hear the truth from people about them, so the value of coaches may increase as people move to higher levels.

Some steps you can take to develop your leadership abilities:

Take stock of your strengths: Don't waste time trying to be something you're not. Become world class in your area of expertise.

Look around for the high performers: See what they're doing. Ask questions. Copy their actions.

Try out leadership skills in other settings: Volunteer in your community. Practicing leadership in other aspects of your life allows you additional opportunities to hone and perfect your skills.

"There are times when a man should be content with what he has, but never with what he is."
—William George Jordan

44

Develop Your People

Leaders cast a significant shadow in their organizations. We have found that employees who have worked for the same boss for several years tend to share not only the strengths but also the weaknesses of their boss. This cuts both ways—if you are an extraordinary boss, your subordinates are likely to develop these skills, but the areas in which they need to improve will also tend to mirror yours.

A powerful tool in your own development process is to develop the people around you. Some leaders view people development as a frill—extraneous to their "real work." However, taking the time to develop people is an important behavior of a leader, not only for what it does for the people he or she helps, but equally for the impact it has on the leader and the organization. Developing others moves you from being an independent professional person, concerned only with yourself, to the role of

the true leader who creates organizational capacity and builds people.

Some of the following strategies will help in your efforts to develop those around you:

1. Set high expectations for leaders. By getting your best leaders to excel, everyone benefits.

2. Build "personal dashboards" to monitor the effectiveness of those around you. How do your people know that they are performing well? If no objective measures exist currently, take the initiative to develop them. Better yet, encourage others to develop those measures for themselves.

3. Involve your leaders as teachers. One of the best ways to learn something is to teach it. Engaging leaders to teach new skills to their groups not only solidifies that knowledge but also builds skills in the leaders and lends credibility to what is being taught.

4. Make development a longer-term process, not an event. We strongly advocate making development part of ongoing work activities rather than a shorter weekend, a weeklong, or even a multiweek program off the job. We are reminded of the executive who asked his boss about attending a 13-week executive development program, to which the boss replied, "If I can spare you for 13 weeks, I can spare you."

5. Celebrate successes. When positive results are achieved, celebrate them. When measures of effectiveness show success, broadcast them widely.

Some good strategies for helping others reach their potential:

Believe in your people: The success of these measures hinges on your beliefs. If you believe your leaders can become extraordinary, they will rise to the challenge.

Expect change to happen sooner rather than later: Leadership is all about change, so if change is not happening, it probably is not working.

Act on your beliefs: Real learning shows up in new behavior. Pick a person. Pick a concept to apply. Start Monday morning.

"The conventional definition of management is getting work done through people, but real management is developing people through work."
—Agha Hasan Abedi

PART 3
MOTIVATING YOUR EMPLOYEES

Your expert skills and talents have gotten you this far. Now, apply the fast facts and quick guidelines in this section to becoming even more successful and effective—as a motivating manager!

With the right set of techniques, you can reawaken and revive the spirit in your organization. Not only that, you can inspire all those around you by creating an environment in which employees will tap their own motivational energy and perform their best work.

It's all about managers creating an environment in which their employees feel passionate about doing their jobs and putting the best of themselves into those jobs.

45

Build a
Motivated Workforce

Here's the million-dollar question: Who would want to be influenced and inspired by you? If you cannot answer this question, then you have no business managing anyone. As a professional speaker and corporate trainer, I have asked this question of thousands of managers and leaders across America and abroad, and you'd be surprised how difficult this question can be for some managers and supervisors to answer. Oftentimes the response is simply a stunned hush.

Here's why being able to answer this question is so important. Managers can't really do anything or be effective in their jobs if their employees aren't motivated to perform well. So as a manager or supervisor, it's imperative that you continually look for ways to engage your people and rouse their enthusiasm and commitment to the organization and its goals.

The fact is that people are motivated to do what is in their best interests. Your goal as a manager,

then, is to help employees identify their welfare with that of the organization. When this happens, employees will naturally feel motivated to work hard, because it is in their best interest to do so.

All this is another way of saying that motivation is intrinsic. It's what drives us to accomplish our desired ends. Whatever we do, it's always because we believe it will fulfill some present or future personal goal or desire.

Contemplate this. When have you been most excited about your work? For most people that excitement comes from being involved with projects that were near and dear to us—projects we took personally, or in which we believed we could really make a difference and accomplish something for ourselves and others. By helping your employees to identify closely with the job they are doing, you will begin to reap the rewards of intrinsic motivation at work.

And when was the last time you thought about really trying to "turn on" your organization? You're the manager, right? Isn't "managing" your job? Yes, but today motivation needs to be everyone's responsibility. As a manager, it is your job to help build a truly "motivating organization," one that inspires employees to do their very best every day. Given that the role you play as a leader and manager of people is one of extreme importance, here are three key points to help build that motivating organization:

Know why your employees would want to be motivated by you: When you can answer this important question, you will be better equipped to engage workers in their jobs more effectively and influence them to act more enthusiastically to meet company goals.

Recognize that real motivation is an inside job: People talk about motivation's being either intrinsic or extrinsic. But it's really only intrinsic, within each of us. What we refer to as extrinsic motivation is really just external factors, like company perks, bonuses, and pay raises, that ultimately affect our intrinsic motivation.

Turn employees on to what's important and meaningful: This requires managers to inspire their followers to be their best, to take risks, to think like entrepreneurs, and to unleash their limitless and synergistic potential.

"Men and women want to do a good job, a creative job, and if they are provided the proper environment, they will do so."

—Bill Hewlett

46

Know What
Drives People

Managers need to know what drives their employees. Do you?

For starters, if you put people in jobs where they can meet their individual needs while doing the work that's important to the organization, you'll have employees who are more motivated to perform at their best.

Managers have to make work a place where employees feel good about themselves and where the work people do helps them to feel good inside as well. When your employees come to work, they can't turn off their human side, in other words, their human nature. Employees' needs don't shift when they walk through the workplace door. To get people to perform at high levels, you must plug into their human side, or their human nature, affirm them, and help them meet their own needs.

Start by paying attention. Watch people doing their jobs. What gets them excited? What turns them

on? What turns them off? Encourage employees to try out their own methods, provided those methods are compatible with effectively getting the job done.

Next, send out an employee survey about attitudes in the workplace and ask for suggestions for improvements. Once you get this feedback, don't ignore the results. Use the findings to make changes that will improve everyone's working conditions, including yours.

Of course, you can't help every employee meet every need. And there are certain dangers in expecting an employee's job, no matter how gratifying, to constitute his or her entire life. However, there are certain steps that all managers can take to help their employees meet some, or even several, of their inner desires that will drive them to do their best work and find greater motivation in the process. Here are three main ways to go about doing this more effectively:

Appreciate everyone's uniqueness: By acknowledging to your staff that everyone is unique, you will be demonstrating that you honor and appreciate the individual talents and differences all employees bring to the organization. And who knows, you might even uncover a diamond in the rough.

Brainstorm for greater fulfillment: One great way to brainstorm and, thereby, motivate workers is to set up employee focus groups. By doing this, you

will begin to discover what employees would like to get from their work. Ask employees to brainstorm ways to make work more fulfilling. Then don't forget to take action and move forward with ideas and suggestions. When you receive employee ideas that are not appropriate, always explain why and hold out for reconsideration at a later time.

Assume that meaningful purpose is important to people: Always assume that things like personal growth and recognition, creativity, and meaningful purpose are as important to your workers as they are to you. Ask employees to describe their ideal job and what they like or don't like about their work and then use what you learn to make work more fulfilling.

"Ultimately, we're talking about redefining the relationship between boss and subordinate."

—Jack Welch

47

Make Employees Feel Like Partners

If you want your employees to be motivated to do their best, and if you want them to be the most valuable asset on your balance sheet, then let them feel and experience ownership in the organization.

The best managers make every employee feel like a business partner. Why? Because when people feel ownership of something, they look out for it, protect it, and pour themselves into it.

One way world-class organizations and their managers help create workplaces alive with entrepreneurial thinking and a sense of ownership (aside from the usual profit sharing and stock options) is to retitle their employees' positions. For example: Starbucks and TDIndustries refer to their employees as *partners*. Guidant, famous maker of pacemakers, uses the term *employee-owners*. And LensCrafters, Marriott, W. L. Gore, Publix Super Markets, and Capital One all call their people *associates*.

Making everyone feel like a partner in the business is one way managers empower their people. Here are some other ways you can do the same:

Encourage entrepreneurial thinking: This goes beyond profit sharing and stock options. It's about the attitude instilled in others by you, the manager. Instilling an entrepreneurial mind-set requires employees to think like business owners, not employees. The term also conveys a sense of feeling joint ownership and caring about the success of the business and happiness of its people. When employees feel like entrepreneurs, they're motivated to take exceptional pride in their work because they are treated like business partners, not hired help.

Explain how the business is run: Help employees better understand what's going on outside the walls of your department. When employees know how they fit in and the difference they make, they can do their work more intelligently. Give employees information about the organization's history to help establish a greater sense of pride and identity. Instruct employees on how to read the company's annual report, if one is available. Point out the CEO's message to help clarify organizational goals, mission, vision, and progress. Encourage employees to identify things they can do to contribute directly to achieving the organization's strategic goals. Then let them act on their ideas.

Help employees feel as if they own the business: If you want your employees to put more of themselves into their work, help them find more of themselves in the work they do. Here's the key: if you want your employees to be motivated to perform at their highest levels, then help them gain more control of their jobs; help them feel as if they belong to a community, and most of all, as if they own the business!

"It's surprising how much you can accomplish, if you don't care who gets the credit."
—Abraham Lincoln

48

Show Employees How the Business Operates

To succeed in today's business environment, your employees need to know far more about the business than just how to do their jobs. They need to know how it operates.

Influential managers must take the responsibility to help workers better understand the entire organization, gain a clearer perspective on just how the business operates, analyze the competition, learn to take risks, and engage in innovative thinking.

As a manager, you understand how your organization operates and manages its finances. That's your job. So you might not realize what it's like to work without knowing how every person and every job impacts the bottom line. When your employees learn how the organization runs and how it spends and brings in the money, they become more motivated to help make a difference.

Start by arranging for a business basics training program for all workers. There are several on the

market that can be customized to your organization's needs. These programs may use a game format to explain how your organization operates and how it makes and loses money. This can be an enjoyable and fun way to teach employees the business of being in business. And here are a few other suggestions to get people moving on understanding business basics:

Talk money: Share the monthly departmental profit-and-loss statements with your employees. This can quickly help workers to better understand how their jobs and specific duties fit into the overall workings of the organization, their neighborhoods, and even their communities. Take time to analyze scenarios that show the impact one person has on the entire organization. This can be a real eye-opener! The point here is to help your employees see how one person's attitude and behavior might directly impact the organization's bottom line, potential pay raises, bonuses, profit sharing, and so on.

Encourage "open-book managing": The idea of *open-book management* has become quite popular. This concept involves sharing the organization's financial data and operational strategies with employees and then showing them specifically what they cost and what value they add to the organization. Some companies go as far as to post everyone's salaries! A good resource for learning about

this approach is the 1992 book *The Great Game of Business*, by Jack Stack. Information is also available on the Internet at http://greatgame.com.

Help people see the big picture: By showing your employees how to see the big picture and understand the monetary domino effect of every action they take, you instill in them an entrepreneurial mind-set that creates a motivated organization. Your purpose here is to develop smarter, more skilled, and highly motivated employees who understand their role in helping the organization succeed, today and into the future. Helping your employees to see the big picture, and not just a myopic view of their specific tasks, can help make that happen.

"Trust—the glue that binds followers and leaders together."

—Warren Bennis

49

Know the Competition

When employees pull together to compete in the marketplace, their level of motivation rises proportionately when they understand just who and what they are competing against. Nothing brings a team together like the challenge of performing at higher levels than its competitors and then helping the organization grow as a result.

Is having your employees know more about the competition dangerous? Possibly—especially when it comes to unveiling such information as employee incentive plans, salaries, and other perks. But remember, the point of having your workers get to know the competition is that you, as the manager, can use this information to take specific steps to make your company a better place to work. The ultimate goal, of course, is to help create a work environment where employees feel motivated by much more than incentive plans or slightly higher wages.

Helping employees to better understand the competition doesn't necessarily require taking a "rah-rah" attitude either, as if organizations were high-school football teams. This is just another way to help your employees get the big picture because your competitors are a part of that picture.

You will get to know your competition by researching what they are doing and then using that information to improve your own organization. In that spirit, here are some ways both you and your employees can learn a bit more about your competitors.

Help employees to compete in the marketplace: Show your employees how to compete more effectively in the marketplace by encouraging them to learn more about your industry and stay current with industry changes. Budget for employee membership in your industry's professional associations and then give people an opportunity to read their trade publications. Encourage employees to copy and distribute industry news, overviews, and relevant case studies (in some cases you may need permission from the publisher to do so). Suggest employees join Internet discussion groups on subjects dealing with your industry and its management in general.

Start competitor files: Put someone in charge of obtaining the competitor's promotional literature;

then have someone investigate their website and obtain a copy of their annual report, if possible. In addition, a competitor file should include copies of advertisements, profiles of top executives, and the organization's awards and recognition. Assign a team to take it all a step further and determine the competition's strengths and weaknesses in the marketplace, market share, and global reach.

Know your competitors and how you measure up against them: A quick and easy way to do this is to have your employees simply ask your customers to evaluate how your organization measures up to the competition. Tell them to be specific. Find out what your customers have to say about your competitor's pricing, customer care programs, product quality, etc. Have employees document the feedback and use this as a basis for internal improvements within your department.

"Next to knowing all about your own business, the best thing is to know all about the other fellow's business."

—John D. Rockefeller

50

Encourage Intelligent Risk-Taking

Have you ever asked yourself, "Why aren't more of my employees willing to take risks?" Perhaps it's because the few times they tried and things went wrong, they were either disciplined or fired. Even when employees succeed at something risky, with a pat on the back for the result, they may also get chastised for taking the initiative. After all, there are channels and chains of command, assigned responsibilities, managers paid to take risks, and so on. Even in more recent years, management has sent out a mixed message to employees: *We want you to feel empowered and take risks—just don't screw up or you're out of here!*

Let's face it: everyone makes mistakes. The best managers know that, but they also recognize that developing a risk-taking mentality is part of helping employees develop an entrepreneurial approach in their work—and that's motivating! So it is important

for you as a manager and leader to support, encourage, and reward intelligent risk-taking behaviors.

The only way to get better is to try new things, and organizations that don't innovate stagnate. They may even go out of business.

So how can you create a culture that encourages employees to take intelligent risks and feel comfortable doing so? Here are some ideas to consider:

Tell employees risk is a four-letter word for success: Creative and calculated risk-taking can improve any organization. That means that managers and supervisors should help employees try new ways of doing their work, of experimenting to make improvements, and encourage and support them in taking those risks. And what if things don't work out as planned? That's OK because it means they're trying new things. And sometimes things don't work out. When employees are allowed to be human and make mistakes, the recognition for having taken the risk is what they'll remember.

Empower employees to take risks: Do this by allowing employees to take an active role in decision making that involves risk. As a leader, you can set the example by trying new things. Demonstrate to employees how to evaluate whether to take a risk. Look for the critical issues, assess opportunities against objective criteria to determine the potential return, and then decide whether the risk is worth it

and if the organization can stand behind whatever results.

Encourage risk-taking behavior as a learned behavior: Risk taking is something we learn over time, one step at a time. Remind your employees that there is risk in much of what we do in our daily lives, whether that's getting married, having a baby, buying a house, changing jobs, buying a new car, or moving to another city. The more risks we learn to take over time and the greater those risks become, the easier it is to take on a risky situation that has potential and payoff for the entire organization and its people.

"Not failure, but low aim, is crime."
—James Russell Lowell

51

Inspire Creative and Innovative Thinking

When you find an organization that survives and thrives over time, it's usually because managers like you have learned how to adapt to their changing circumstances and sometimes even keep ahead of the changes taking place around them. Managers who encourage creativity and innovative thinking among their people are natural-born motivators.

Start by addressing and eliminating any fears employees may have about creative thinking. Some people, for example, don't think they're capable of being creative. Others tend to focus on areas of practicality, analyzing and judging ideas as quickly as they arise. Let your employees know that it's time to lighten up and not to assume that something won't work because nobody's tried it. Have your employees suspend critical judgment when someone presents what may seem to be an off-the-wall or different kind of idea in comparison with what's been proposed in the past. Have employees concentrate on

how they can make new ideas work and not what's wrong with them.

Motivating managers pride themselves on providing a free and open environment that inspires employees to offer whatever ideas and suggestions may occur to them—no matter how "impractical" they may seem at first. It's in this type of environment where employees will feel motivated to stretch themselves and use their imaginations to help the organization (and themselves) succeed. Here are some ways to encourage creativity:

Think big. Think virtual: Today, employee brainstorming can be done over long distances through the use of cyberspace auditoriums and virtual conference rooms. Virtual meetings are proliferating and prove that groups can function just as effectively and synchronously in cyberspace as they can in the office conference room down the hall. Just think, it is now possible for your employees to hash out ideas with colleagues in the UK, get input from other team members in Burlington, Vermont, go over a game plan before a meeting with other employees in Honolulu, and kibitz with a new member of the team in Melbourne, Australia.

Use tools for creative and innovative thinking: Begin by setting aside time to brainstorm with employees and investigate innovative and creative new approaches and ideas. Not only should you sup-

port innovative thinking, but as the manager, you should also help implement new ideas. Make books available to your employees on the subject of creativity, such as *A Whack on the Side of the Head* by Roger von Oech, *Thinkertoys* by Michael Michalko, or *How to Think Like Einstein: Simple Ways to Break the Rules and Discover Your Hidden Genius* by Scott Thorpe. Through special announcements, newsletters, e-mails, and day-to-day conversations, praise the innovation of your team.

Emphasize positive aspects of innovative solutions: Continually emphasize the positive aspects of innovative solution finding and the disadvantages of always doing the same things in the same way. Refrain from penalizing anyone for trying something new that may end up a big mistake. Instead, encourage others to learn from their mistakes. It's your responsibility to encourage freedom of expression and congratulate those who possess unique, one-of-a-kind creativity and out-of-the-box thinking skills.

"There is nothing that is a more certain sign of insanity than to do the same thing over and over and expect the results to be different."
—Albert Einstein

52

Affirm the Link Between Motivation and Performance

As a leader, you need to know that there is a direct link between employee motivation and employee performance. In fact, it can be a positively outrageous connection depending on the culture of your organization and the enthusiasm and excitement your company's culture instills in its people.

Perhaps you've seen companies like Disney, Saturn, SAS Institute, Southwest Airlines, Starbucks, USAA, Rosenbluth International, and The Ritz Carlton (just to name a few) that always seem to go the extra mile for their customers' satisfaction and happiness and whose employees are upbeat and glad to be working there. And without even thinking about it, you somehow know there is a direct connection between how those employees perform on the job and just how motivated they are about their work. It's practically palpable—you can feel it! That's because these employees are motivated to do these things, and it shows up in the quality of their work.

In other words, if you don't think motivation and performance are connected, think again. Here are three important factors to consider when it comes to linking the motivation of your people to higher levels of performance and productivity:

Know the impact you're having on people: All managers occasionally feel as though they are having little or no impact on the motivation of their employees. Let's face it: you can't always change or control certain factors that affect your employees' enthusiasm for their jobs. Some things, such as working conditions, specific assignments, salaries, and benefits, you can provide, but other factors can simply be out of your control. Still, as the manager, you have a direct impact on linking employee motivation to performance. Learn some of the effective techniques that are working for other managers and then try them when they seem appropriate for your employees. Be willing to commit to a strategy so that employees don't feel your approach is simply a "flavor-of-the-week" series of gimmicks. You'll be pleasantly surprised to find that you can influence your employees' motivation and improve their productivity and attitudes when you try appropriate, innovative techniques and use them with your own personal style of leadership, business sense, and people skills.

Make sure employees know what performance is: Never assume that your employees will automatically know what you mean by "performance." It's your responsibility to clearly define performance standards for them. You need to think of performance in your own terms and then clearly and precisely explain what that means to your employees. Only then will you be capable of linking performance to motivation successfully.

Tell people what's expected of them and be specific: Here are the questions every manager must be able to answer for every employee: "What's expected of me?" "What is my role as a part of the group and the organization?" "What's considered unacceptable performance?" "What must I do to reach your standards of performance?" Be explicit! The more detailed and explicit the expectations, the greater the chance the employee will meet or exceed them.

"No person who is enthusiastic about his work has anything to fear from life."

—Samuel Goldwyn

53

Help Employees Achieve Greater Performance

In the beginning lessons of this section, we focused on helping employees become intrinsically motivated. We also focused on how you as a manager or supervisor can more effectively influence the forces that compel others to do the things they do to the best of their talent. In this lesson and the preceding one, we're shifting our focus to getting employees to take *direction* and then stretch themselves in order to turn motivation into stronger performance and higher productivity. Here are some ways to consider doing this:

Stretch people beyond their perceived limits: Take your employees above and beyond the status quo of just doing the same job the same way. Make their work challenging, and help them to see the bigger picture and the part they play in it. They may resist if they feel that higher expectations are being imposed on them. Let your employees know that

you are simply trying to help them stretch and grow for their own benefit. They will love you for it! You can do this by helping them set individual performance goals that exceed the existing requirements of their jobs. Further, when you can explain how their work adds value to the organization and how what they do affects the work of others, your employees can begin to figure out different ways to improve and grow their talents on their own.

Set standards and be clear: Identify those standards for a particular job and be specific about the outcomes that characterize outstanding as well as unacceptable performance. Involve your employees in doing this. Employees who are involved in developing standards are more likely to discuss the obstacles that might impede their efforts along the way, allowing you to handle those issues head-on before things get out of hand. Involved employees are also far more likely to understand the standards and reasons behind them, so you won't have to work so hard to communicate these standards again and again. And these employees are far more likely to accept such guidelines for success and be motivated to meet them to the best of their ability.

Define employees' scope of responsibility: Make sure everyone understands who is responsible for each job activity. When employees know their roles, this reduces confusion and gives them a better

sense of how they might work with their fellow employees to meet their individual objectives. Once you've done this, you've set up the next step, which is to help employees broaden the scope of their responsibilities and open new opportunities for them. As an employee responds, you might want to suggest that he or she assume greater decision-making authority on a certain project. But be careful. Your goal is not to heap more work on the shoulders of your employees. They need to know that you genuinely appreciate their efforts and want to provide them with the opportunity to learn more and excel on the job. You want your employees to feel that it is in their best interests to go the extra mile.

"All of us do not have equal talent, but all of us should have an equal opportunity to develop our talent."

—John F. Kennedy

54

Get Employees to Buy Into Your Ideas— and Theirs

The more input an employee can provide about the job he or she is expected to perform, the more likely the employee is to buy into your ideas for how to do it well. When they know you actually care about their performance and are willing to listen to their ideas for improvement, they'll be motivated to accept your suggestions as well.

The term "buy-in" is one that every manager uses at one time or another, but often not in the same way. If you think that getting your employees to buy into a program means somehow compelling them to accept it, you're likely to run into problems. Employees truly buy in when they decide to invest their individual abilities and energies, as if they were business owners making a financial investment in a joint venture. So give your employees the opportunity to get involved. If you do, they will be motivated to buy into higher standards of performance

on every level. Here you can contemplate other ways this can be carried out successfully:

Give employees a role in raising workplace standards or performance: When you include your employees in raising workplace standards or performance levels, they'll eagerly share with you their ideas and suggestions for improving the process. Keep in mind that almost all employees have a strong desire to play a role in raising their own performance expectations and, when allowed to do so, will set the bar higher than you might have anticipated.

Document what you and your employees agree on: Develop a written list of performance standards for meeting and exceeding the expectations you've agreed upon with your employees. Remember, you want your employees to continue to stretch, yet you want to be certain they can attain their goals. This is key in staying highly motivated. Next, be specific about what it's going to take to actually reach those goals, in each area or each job function. Document those expectations and then give a copy to every employee. At your next employee performance review or upon completion of a project, this document will serve as the basis for you and the employee to discuss and measure what was accomplished. Remember, what gets measured is what he or she will be most motivated to do.

Plan a course of action, then get moving: Once the standards are set, review the specific tasks of each person's job. Identify and discuss the areas in which each person is skilled and qualified. Plan a course of action and delegate based on each employee's experience and level of competence. Next, let each employee know that once he or she has started the project and gained greater insight into the intricacies of the job, you will be willing at that point to revise the expectations accordingly. Be sure to keep the goals challenging, yet realistic. Now get moving, but take time to observe and follow up. Don't wait until the end of a project to check in with your employees. Following up is an important way you give your employees the feedback they need concerning their performance as it's happening. It's also a great way to demonstrate that your job as manager is to help each employee succeed—reinforcing their motivation to perform.

"Every manager knows how to count, but smart managers know what counts."

—Anonymous

55

Be Clear—and Consistent—About Rewards and Recognition

Let your employees know up front what to expect if they meet or exceed the standards of excellence you've set for them with their help. Be clear about potential rewards for hitting those goals. In other words, let employees know what's in it for them, then plan on them succeeding beyond your wildest imagination. Sure, it may be less expensive for the organization if employees fall slightly short on meeting your expectations, because then you'd be saving on those rewards. But the smartest managers know that success, even when it entails additional expense, breeds greater success and motivation among the ranks.

When your employees do hit the target and meet a standard you've set for them, reward them immediately. Never stall. By doing this, you help

employees directly connect the reward with the behavior and higher performance they've attained.

Never make a promise without a plan to deliver. When that happens, it sends a message to employees that you can't be trusted and that you really don't have faith in them. On the other hand, don't make the promise of rewards the main reason for employees to perform. What you want is for employees to know that rewards are recognition of a job well done and not simply the goal of doing the work.

Think about the people behind the performance. Rewards and recognition should fit the achievement, but also the employee. If you want to reward a telemarketer, for example, he or she may appreciate a weekend getaway with meals and accommodations provided. However, if you are rewarding a traveling sales rep, such a prize may not excite someone who spends a great deal of time in hotels and restaurants anyway.

Here are some positive forms of reinforcement that aren't expensive and will help get the point across to your employees that you want to recognize a job well done:

Create greater autonomy: This tells employees that you trust them to make decisions that affect their work. It also conveys a sense of additional responsibility.

Increase visibility within the organization: Send an e-mail or memo to others publicly recognizing the good work of someone. When you help increase the visibility of an employee who's done a good job, you're reinforcing that good work by your praise and recognition. If it's in the budget, another way to appreciate a job well done is to provide that person with additional resources, such as a new computer system, software, an assistant, or monies for books and seminars.

Showcase success: Showcasing success often calls for special recognition, like a framed certificate or an engraved plaque or trophy. Sometimes managers like to showcase success on a quarterly basis with "Walk-the-Talk" awards or gift certificates for the team. In some cases, managers let the employees themselves showcase their hard work and special accomplishments by asking them to present a special case study at a prestigious management conference or leadership meeting.

"There are two things people want more than sex and money . . . recognition and praise."
—Mary Kay Ash

56

Always Expect the Best from Employees

It's actually pretty natural, and almost unavoidable, for managers to form expectations of their workers. Research has found that in an organization, our expectations of others can be tied directly to productivity, profitability, and yes—motivation! If you have high expectations of your employees, you will possess a powerful and effective tool for improving performance and motivation within your organization.

Performance is often a matter of expectations. Managers and supervisors form expectations of others, which then influence how they interact with those people. If you don't expect much from your employees, they will sense that and perform poorly. Why? Because your expectations of them affect their desire to do well. The point is that people naturally try to live up to our expectations of them, or live down to them, whatever the case may be. So expect the best from your employees and don't be sur-

prised if that's exactly what you get! Here are some ideas on how managers can get the best from their people:

Get what you ask for: Expectations influence behavior. Simply put, if you expect the best from your employees, you will more than likely get it—over and over again. This is especially true if you treat employees as if they can perform and you give them the information and tools they need. That makes it easy for them to feel motivated and deliver what you (and now they) expect.

Take advantage of the Pygmalion effect: That's the tendency of people to act in ways that are consistent with their expectations. Employee performance improves greatly when managers are told beforehand that they are going to be leading an exceptional group of high-potential workers. Because those managers then tend to treat these employees as if they are capable of superior performance, they deliver. Use the Pygmalion effect, by showing that you are committed to your people and by doing the following: create a high-performance environment, share the rewards of successful performance, and inspire others to higher-level performance.

Create a high-performing, high-producing environment: If you really want to tap into the true motivation within your employees, you must deliberately create an environment that's conducive to higher

levels of employee performance. That means that everyone is clear and focused about the organization's objectives, that the work is stimulating and challenging, that people feel appreciated and respected, that people have the resources they need, and that people help and support one another without being asked to do so.

"Leadership is performance. You have to be conscious of your behavior, because everyone else is."

—Carly Fiorina

57

Fire Up Successful Performance

If you really want to fire up successful performance in your people, then you'll need to inspire them to reach those higher levels of performance and productivity. Great leaders are often inspirational. They seem to have a knack for fostering optimism and belief in a better tomorrow. As a manager or supervisor, you too can create an environment that encourages people to climb to the next level of achievement, satisfaction, and personal excellence.

Do all that you can to show your employees that your actions are meaningful and sincere when it comes to helping them do their best work.

Consider the following strategies: 1. Ask for everyone's input, ideas, and suggestions about the current work environment and how it can be improved. Then publish a plan and let your people put it into action. Now that's motivating! 2. Emphasize your own personal commitment to your team. In other words, you too must be fired up about your

work. Always praise the commitment of your staff. 3. Connect the success of your team to the success of the organization. When you practice these strategies, you'll be helping to ensure that management values its people and wants to take actions that will benefit both employees and the organization. Here are some additional ways to fire up employees:

Share rewards: An important goal of any motivation program is to help employees feel that the work itself is the reward. Managers reinforce our natural human motivation when they arrange for employees to enjoy rewards that result from their work. So share the rewards with all those who have contributed to the organization's success. For example, when an employee or group of employees improves a process or saves the company money, share those benefits with them. The plan may include a percentage of the savings or a flat bonus.

Recognize and praise them: Besides pay, there are other ways to share in the rewards of successful performance. For example, you may be amazed at how employees respond to a simple compliment for work well done. It's best to compliment a person face-to-face, then follow up by sending him or her a letter or e-mail of appreciation. And in this day and age of technology-generated correspondence, a handwritten card or thank-you note is valued even

more. Remember to always be specific in your compliments.

Train, train, train: Nothing fires up successful performance among employees more than training. Training people sends out a clear message that says, "You are worth this investment!" Give employees special learning opportunities, both inside and outside of the organization. Always encourage ongoing personal and professional development and watch motivation soar! When employees are exposed to training programs, seminars, e-learning, etc., it tells them that management really values their performance and wants to help them to continually improve their skills. When you do this, make sure you also give employees immediate opportunities to use their new skills. This way, the training pays off quickly and people take what they learned seriously.

"The shortest and best way to make your fortune is to let people see that it is in their interests to promote yours."

—Jean de La Bruyere

58

Offer Incentives and Morale Boosters

One way managers are discovering how to enrich the workplace is to boost the benefits of working there. The days when benefits packages included nothing more than a health plan and dental coverage are over. Managers like you are getting more and more creative when it comes to providing their employees with uniquely-their-own incentives and morale boosters that contribute to an ever-changing, exciting, and motivating work environment.

Take a fast lesson from some of these world-class companies that are designing their own employee incentives and providing the motivating perks that result in higher performance levels and happier employees!

■ Goldman Sachs, New York: When employees work late into the night, the Wall Street firm sends them home in a limo at no cost.

■ Valassis Communications, Livonia, Michigan: Employees receive "wheels on loan" if their car is

in the shop, "you've got it maid" discounts on maid service, and infant car seats for brand-new parents.

- MBNA, Wilmington, Delaware: Say "I do" and the firm gives generous wedding gifts to employees, including limo service on their wedding day, plus $500 and a week of vacation.

- WRQ, Inc., Seattle, Washington: Quirky but true, this integration software provider offers employees a nap room with futons.

- J. M. Smucker, Orrville, Ohio: The famous jam maker enriches the environment with ongoing job rotations to keep employees motivated and interested.

- REI, Kent, Washington: New dads get two weeks of paid leave to be with their babies.

- Dell Computer, Round Rock, Texas: Everyone gets a week off at Christmas and 10 paid days a year for personal use.

Here are some thoughts on how you can be creative with incentives:

Be flexible with employees: Did you know that helping your employees strike a life balance keeps employee motivation high? Did you also know that the most requested perk on the job is flexibility? Here's the kind of flexibility employees ask for the most: telecommuting, flex schedules, job sharing, compressed workweek (10-hour days, four days a week), reduction in summer work hours, and time off to take care of personal matters when necessary.

Motivate without money: Yes, it's possible to motivate workers with little or no money. Here are some ideas: post a thank-you note on an employee's office door, have a day when managers wash their employees' cars, answer someone's telephone for a day, hold morale-building meetings to celebrate successes, leave a card for a lunch date at the employee's discretion, walk around with dinner gift certificates that can be handed out on the spot, assign a parking spot for an entire month, give two consecutive Fridays off, buy someone flowers, make a contribution to someone's favorite charity.

Walk the talk: Be the role model for what you expect in others. Also, convey your enthusiasm and remind others that problems can be overcome. Always recognize people who conquer obstacles to achieve results. Focus on the positive side of new ideas. Meet with people individually or in groups, especially when morale is low. Express your optimism and faith in the team. Concentrate on the small but significant wins, not just the big successes. Make work fun and celebrate a lot!

"People want to feel what they do makes a difference."

—Frances Hesselbein

59

Give Your Power Away

Let your people be powerful. If you really want to pump them up, then prepare to give your power away.

Even before empowerment became a management buzzword, smart managers were already familiar with the basic principle: when workers feel strong, confident, and capable, they can accomplish more. Those same managers also know that when workers feel unappreciated or insignificant to the overall operation, and when they lack responsibility and authority, they tend to perform down to low management expectations. They also tend to whine and complain a lot.

That's why the most motivating managers give their power away over and over again. Sure it's unconventional, and many managers resist doing this because they like holding all the power. But think about it for a minute. You're not there as a manager to hold the power. That's just a resource—

a means toward an end. Your responsibility as a motivating manager is to use your authority to get results and to help your employees perform better. So if giving your power away helps to improve performance, then by all means, that's exactly what you should be doing.

When you give your power away, you are allowing your employees to share your responsibility and authority. They find greater motivation in their work, and little by little you will free yourself from the burden of using whips, carrots, or other extrinsic forces to try to influence them and their behaviors. Here are some additional lessons to achieving that same goal:

Help employees accept responsibility for motivation: When employees rely on themselves to stay motivated, rather than on others, they're accepting self-responsibility. And when they accept responsibility for themselves, they understand that they also have responsibility for their success. To encourage self-responsibility for motivation, give employees carte blanche responsibility for achieving a specific task or project to make it their own, and give the full authority to do it their way. This will unleash tremendous energy and motivation among your people. Remember, one of the greatest de-motivators is to assign responsibility to someone and then turn around and tell the person how to do the job. Top managers won't make this mistake.

Let the people take the power: Smart managers know the importance of releasing the power within each employee so that he or she can do the best work. When your people take the power, you will be giving them the authority and responsibility to do their jobs efficiently and effectively, on their own. "People have the power" has long been the credo at the famous jeans maker Levi Strauss & Co. and has helped sustain the company through the fringed '60s and bell-bottomed '70s, to the total reinvention of the jeans culture at the turn of the century.

Redefine your role as manager: To do this, start by enlarging every employees' circle of influence. Then increase signature authority whenever possible. Don't let employees feel restricted by their titles or positions. Everyone's a leader. Define jobs more broadly, leaving room for creativity and autonomy. Eliminate cumbersome employee rules and policies. And always support good judgment and common sense. Remember Nordstrom's employee handbook, which simply states: *Rule #1: Use your good judgment in all situations. There will be no additional rules.*

"If you want someone to do a good job, give them a good job to do."
—Frederick Herzberg

60

Encourage Accountability at All Times

What's the best way to encourage accountability among your employees? By helping them understand and appreciate the role they play in the big organizational picture.

There's a saying that should make every manager think: "No individual raindrop ever considers itself responsible for the flood." And on a more positive note: "No individual raindrop ever can take credit for the flowers." It's lots of raindrops working together, each making its contribution.

People who do extraordinary things do so because they are accountable to themselves first. It's definitely not just to get a raise or promotion. What pushes each and every one of us to go the extra mile or to climb the highest mountain? It's self-motivation—motivation that comes from within one's heart and mind, motivation that holds each person accountable. There truly is no greater

human force. Here are some ideas for plugging into that:

Encourage employees to believe in themselves: Whatever actions you may take as a manager, your ultimate goal should be to help all of your employees believe in themselves and believe that they can accomplish what they set out to do. Help your employees accept a sense of accountability for their work. This will not only guide them but inspire them as well. When a woman by the name of Ffyona Campbell set out to walk 16,088 kilometers across Africa from Cape Town to Tangiers, it amazed everyone. When asked why she was doing it, she replied, "Because I said I would." When asked whom she said it to, she answered, "Myself." Ffyona believed in herself, and it was that inner belief and confidence that inspired her to take on the more treacherous terrain on foot and alone. Her self-motivated and extraordinary efforts earned her the title "The Greatest Walker of Them All."

Help others bridge the gap to achieving goals: Staying self-motivated and accepting responsibility is the bridge between setting goals and reaching them. It's always the driving force behind people's achievements. Here are two effective ways to help your employees bridge the gap to achieve their goals. One, help employees face fear. Encourage employees to openly discuss their fears and what

scares them most and then take action in spite of those fears. When employees start moving toward their goals, their fears and anxieties will soon dissipate and confidence will begin to strengthen. Two, help employees focus on the end result. Help them visualize what success might look like and then drive toward it.

Hold employees accountable: Being accountable means taking responsibility for your actions and their outcomes. Real accountability goes beyond the performance of a task. It means they feel responsible for their work and for the results they achieve. Here are some tips for holding your employees accountable: develop a list of mutually acceptable performance criteria; connect expectations to employee reviews and put expectations in writing beforehand; establish rewards for success and consequences when a job is done poorly; make excellence the only option and demonstrate a low tolerance for mediocrity.

"We must exchange the philosophy of excuse—what I am is beyond my control—for the philosophy of responsibility."
—Barbara Jordan

61

Build Trust for a Better Tomorrow

Motivation is partly based on a vision of hope—the hope for success from our efforts and for a better future for ourselves. In other words, *what life could be*. When we believe in the possibilities, for ourselves and for our employees, a brighter tomorrow opens up.

As a manager, one of the most important things you can do for your people is to give them hope. Not just hope by itself, but hope that offers direction, believability, and genuine encouragement. When people have a good sense about their future, it reinforces their enthusiasm and commitment to the work in which they're involved. It's motivating. It says there is a payoff to the individual for doing well. Here are other ways managers work toward building a better tomorrow for their employees:

Understand the phenomenon of human potential: Potential is something that may or may not be fully developed in people. Whatever people's potential

might be, they won't know unless they have a chance to develop it. And that's where you as a leader come in. Take time to rent and watch the movie *Phenomenon*, starring John Travolta. The film sends a profound message about our untapped potential that is poignantly delivered near the end of the movie by Travolta's character, George Malley, who says, "I am what everyone can be. I'm the possibility, and anyone can get there." You can help unleash that possibility by encouraging people to try new things and take on new responsibilities.

Build trust: Trust is an essential element in managing people and building a high-performing organization. It's the foundation upon which all relationships are built. According to Tom Peters, "Technique and technology are important. But adding trust is the issue of the decade." Peters suggests that managers must take a "high-tech and high-trust" approach, putting the issue of trust at the top of the agenda and treating it like a "hard issue," not a "soft issue." If employees feel you don't trust them to do their jobs correctly, they'll be reluctant to do much without your approval. On the other hand, when they feel trusted that you can believe they'll do the right things, they'll naturally want to do things well and be deserving of your trust.

Show employees they are worthy of your trust: When you put your trust in others, you're sending a

strong message that says, "I think you're trustworthy." This tells people that you have faith in their ability and competence and you believe they've got what it takes to do the job. Trust is a prerequisite for building confidence in people. Some managers don't discuss the issue of trust, or they use the word in very limited contexts, often almost negatively. For example, "Now, Matt, I trust you to do this right" means "Don't screw up, Matt." And, "We're trusting you to do your best, Jane" really sends the message, "We're not sure what's happening here, so we're just hoping that you can somehow pull this off." These, so-called, expressions of "trust" are unlikely to reassure Matt or Jane. Show your trust in employees by allowing them to think for themselves, ask questions, and make their own decisions. Those are the "real" expressions of trust employees can sense and believe. This is how smart managers show employees that they are worthy of their trust.

"The trust that we put in ourselves makes us feel trust in others."

—François de la Rochefoucauld

62

Boost Morale

Morale has to do with the enthusiam and commitment people bring to their jobs every day. It affects their motivation to perform. Low morale = low motivation. High morale = high motivation. It may not be quite that simple, but there is a direct correlation between morale and motivation.

Every organization depends on the relationships that its people have among one another. A high-morale workplace needs to be built on the concepts of trust and integrity. But it's not enough for you to trust your employees. They've got to trust you as well. Employees want to believe that their managers are looking out for their best interests. And the way that happens is for them to experience it every day on the job. The great thing about this is that the employees (nearly all of them, anyway) will want to reciprocate, looking out for your and the organization's best interests.

Remember that your people are your greatest and most valuable resource. You may have hired

them for their aptitudes, but the key to higher performance lies in their attitudes. The more you can do to build a high-morale workplace, while instilling trust in your employees, the more motivated they will be. Let's look at some ways you can do this throughout your organization:

Do what you say you will do: Be short on promises and long on fulfillment. Nothing builds trust more than having your words and actions match. Good intentions aren't enough. Tell your employees you care, and then match that up with deeds that demonstrate it every day. High morale will follow naturally.

Let integrity be the highest form of intelligence in your organization: Integrity has been described by some as the highest form of human intelligence. Integrity is not only an expansion of human honesty and trustworthiness; it is what remains when we strip away all of our credentials and reputation. It's our moral fiber and conscience, our principal beliefs and values. And it is also another characteristic of the high-morale workplace.

Be truthful and show your human side: Do you believe in what you are conveying to others? Are you true to yourself? Do you lead by example and do the right things in accordance with your values? You can't be a good manager if you're acting in ways that are inconsistent with who you really are and what

you believe. Be truthful with people and don't be afraid to show your human side. It's OK to share your mistakes, your hopes, and your dreams. Be down-to-earth and straightforward with people. Employees will respect and appreciate your honesty and your humanity—two more characteristics of the high-morale workplace.

"We must do more than simply do things right—we must also do the right things."
—Excerpt from "Our Values," Pfizer Pharmaceutical

63

Make It Fun to Make It Motivating

The data are in and the results are clear! There is a direct correlation between fun on the job and employee productivity, creativity, morale, satisfaction, retention, and, yes, you guessed it, profitability—not to mention greater customer satisfaction and a host of other benefits. For example, having fun at work helps to alleviate stress and tension, improve communication, ease conflict, unite people, eliminate boredom and fatigue, and create lots of positive energy!

In other words, people who work in an enjoyable and fun-filled workplace come to see their jobs as a place to fulfill many different needs, reinforcing their motivation to perform at a higher level.

You can certainly train people to do just about anything. But the key to real success and to leading a motivated workforce is having people who really *want* to do their jobs and who love to come to work. These people enlighten the workplace and

energize their coworkers. That's the big difference having fun at work can make. If you think you're ready to take life a little less seriously and begin enjoying the benefits of a more fun and happier workplace, consider the following:

Instigate the "fun"damentals of motivation: Let's say you're convinced that it's good business to loosen up and create a fun and more enjoyable workplace—great! But suppose you just don't know how to go about it? Here are a few tips for setting up the "fun"damentals of motivation where you work:

- Laugh with people, not at them.
- Lighten up. Don't take yourself too seriously.
- Think with a sense of humor.
- Adopt a fun and playful attitude.
- Plan to have a good time every single day.
- Help others see the lighter side of things.

Need more help? Check out *301 Ways to Have Fun at Work* by Dave Hemsath and Leslie Yerkes and *Get Weird!* by John Putzier.

Know the connection between fun and the bottom line: Do you want to reduce absenteeism, promote greater job satisfaction, boost employee performance, increase productivity, and suffer less downtime? By your encouraging a fun work environment, these will be just a few of the bottom-line benefits you can expect. Also, take time to study some of the world's most fun organizations. Here are a few fun

companies to check out: Rock and Roll Hall of Fame and Museum (Cleveland, Ohio), Virgin Management Limited, Southwest Airlines, Disney, and Ben & Jerry's. And here's one more tidbit to consider: a survey of business school deans and business executives revealed that humor plays a significant part in the operation of a healthy, successful business.

Recognize the power of fun: Fun, laughter, humor—it's all cleansing. It unites us with everyone else who is having fun. It can make it nearly impossible to feel lonely or left out. When we share a laugh, we enjoy the laugh, but we also enjoy the sharing. Fun is motivating because of the pleasure it creates. So when your employees are feeling a bit down, stressed, tired, or just not in the mood to work up to their abilities, a laugh can make a big difference.

"All I wanna do is have some fun. I got a feeling I'm not the only one."

—Sheryl Crow

64

Attack De-Motivators Head-On

As a manager, you directly or indirectly impact your employees' self-confidence, their desires, their long-term interests, and their overall ability to love what they do for a living. That's a lot of pressure on any manager to get it right.

This section is full of tips and guidelines to help you positively influence the motivation of your employees. But, let's face it: we live in demanding and increasingly negative times. No matter how supportive, motivating, or encouraging you may be as a manager, you're no doubt constantly facing circumstances that negatively influence the motivation of your employees.

So how do you as a leader build and maintain hope in the midst of influences that threaten to de-motivate? Simple. You attack the de-motivators head-on. Concentrate on putting your energy into what you *can* do, rather than dwelling on de-motivating circumstances and making their effects

worse. If you do this, you will be better able to combat doom and gloom and confront the adversity that negatively affects the motivation of your employees.

Remember that de-motivators are factors that deflate the motivation bubble. They can be events, management decisions, disappointments, a lack of praise and rewards, and so on. Zeroing in on what's causing your people to feel deflated can help you to attack the de-motivators and keep them at bay. There are three specific areas you need to be aware of in which you can build organizational strength so that your employees can better handle de-motivating situations:

Hire for the best fit: The best way to counter de-motivation is to prevent it, and sometimes the problem can be with the people you hire. There are folks who tend to get de-motivated quite easily or who are just negative in one way or another. Since you can't count on overcoming a person's psychological issues, it's best to avoid hiring such people. Put some time into screening out candidates who seem likely to suffer from motivation problems.

Hold on to your best employees by creating an environment that offers lots of feedback and builds confidence: Losing good people is a definite de-motivator. To avoid that, give your employees accurate and honest feedback and praise. Feedback strengthens employees and builds confidence, even when it's

corrective. Ask your employees how they would like to receive feedback from you. You'll be establishing a foundation that helps to avoid surprises and minimize de-motivating discomfort. Managers who create an environment rich with honest feedback and praise encourage employee cooperation and trust and higher levels of performance and productivity.

Protect people's dignity and self-respect at all times: One of the greatest de-motivators for employees is having their dignity undermined. Create an environment that encourages employees to respect one another. Some tips for doing this: never criticize an employee in front of others; offer corrective feedback only in private; never point a finger at someone—it's demeaning and unprofessional; never use a condescending tone of voice; never attack someone personally; focus on professional behaviors and performance only; and finally, if you expect others to respect your sense of dignity, you should show them the same respect.

"There's only one way to know how strong employee motivation is throughout your company—ask the people who actually work there. If the de-motivators are seeping in, then it's time to put the kibosh on any and all de-motivators in a hurry!"

—Anonymous

65

Put Heart and Soul into Your Team

In this global society in which we work, we tend to first learn about such business things as operations, finance, marketing strategy, productions, customer service, and so on. That can mean that as managers, we sometimes neglect the fact that, at their very core, organizations are about people and the relationships they develop in working together.

It's the people and the teams they create that turn individual employees into a community of people working together to achieve individual and shared goals. And it's because managers care about their people that this actually becomes possible. There's a saying that goes: "People don't care how much you know, until they know how much you care." Why? Because when you care about your employees, you create an atmosphere where they care about you and about each other. It turns on their motivation to perform well and to want to improve.

If you genuinely care about your employees and show them, you'll be meeting their basic need to be cared about. You'll be motivating them with heart and soul. And it's that special feeling of reassurance that will help them find greater motivation to work harder and smarter.

Inspire motivated teamwork: Making a difference and collaborating with others to achieve a goal are two of the most powerful motivators for accomplishing challenging work. Put these two things together and you have the potential for a high-performing team. Do all you can to show your appreciation for the contributions an employee makes and by being a leader who promotes and facilitates teamwork.

Lead from the heart: The word "encouragement" has as its root the Latin word *cor*, which means "heart." When you encourage employees, you actually give them heart. You lead them with feeling. When Barbara Walters interviewed General Norman Schwarzkopf following the Gulf War, she asked him how he would most like to be remembered. His answer was from the heart: *That he loved his family. That he loved his troops. And that they loved him.* Motivating leadership is an affair of the heart, and such leaders care about their employees and their organizations. Employees will naturally and positively respond to this.

Encourage team spirit: Smart managers know that team spirit unifies. Transforming a group of individuals into a team provides unification and a common sense of interest and direction. Keep in mind that as the manager, you are setting the tone. Your actions and attitudes directly affect the environment in which your team must perform. Here are some suggestions for encouraging team spirit:

- Give teams a clearly defined goal and purpose.
- Let the team make its own rules.
- Encourage fun and a sense of humor on the job.
- Give employees the authority to make decisions and act on them.
- Be supportive. Do what you promise to do.
- Let the team find solutions to its problems without intervening.
- Allow team members to make financial decisions and create their own budgets.
- Expect ups and downs. Some phases of a project will run more smoothly than others.
- Let the team set up a reward system.

"Coming together is a beginning; keeping together is progress; working together is success."
—Henry Ford

66

Unleash the Power of Human Potential

Did you know that your brain's capacity is practically unfathomable? In terms of its intricacies and power, the brain surpasses even the latest technologies. It can actually process up to 30 billion bits of information per second through the equivalent of more than 6,000 miles of computer wiring. The fuel that fires up your brain is pretty simple: oxygen in the blood and a little glucose, and bingo, you've got energy. And without energy, there can be no synergy in your organization.

When people feel tired or listless, they don't accomplish nearly as much as they're capable of accomplishing. When you work on increasing your employees' energy, you help them move toward a better life working together. That's what synergy really means—working together. It's a simple, natural concept that managers like you are learning to adopt in their business practices. As management experts stress the importance of "smart work" and "intellectual capital," managers and supervisors are realizing

the importance of these synergistic qualities and the benefits they can produce within the team's structure.

This section has given you lots of ways for getting the best from your employees. The guidelines and tips offered were meant to get you thinking—thinking about the potential that lies within you and all of your employees, the phenomenal power of all that intelligence, creativity, curiosity, and energy. As a manager and leader, it is imperative that you make the most of all that potential around you. The results will be well worth your efforts, as the synergy you develop will keep growing, building, and motivating for a long time to come. In the words of Ralph Waldo Emerson, "Make the most of yourself . . . for that is all there is of you." Here are some more ways that managers unleash the power of human potential in their employees:

Train 'em: The saying goes, "Knowledge is power." It is not. What is powerful is how knowledge is used. So what kind of training programs do you provide to help employees gain new knowledge and use it effectively? Training helps employees improve their skills and performance—and it shows in yet another way that you care about them.

Coach 'em: Once you've invested in your employees' learning and development, it's time to start a coaching program. You go to a lot of trouble to maintain your computers and other equipment. But when it comes to sustaining the motivation of

your employees, it's easy to forget that they too must be "maintained." Coaching is an effective way to maintain employee motivation. Here's the definition of the word "coach": "Someone who lends experience, encouragement, and understanding to inspire someone to his or her best performance."

Love 'em: As the hit song by Tina Turner asks, "What's love got to do with it?" The answer: everything! The truly successful manager is a manager who actually loves his or her people and demonstrates this love by encouraging a loving atmosphere on the job. Simply put, "love" in this context means that you're concerned about your people and their success, that you feel glad when they succeed, and that you are willing to help them out and go the extra distance when they need it. The feeling of a loving and caring work environment is the essence of inspiring motivated teamwork.

> **"Work can provide the opportunity for spiritual and personal, as well as financial, growth. If it doesn't, then we're wasting far too much of our lives on it."**
>
> —James A. Autry, *Love and Profit: The Art of Caring Leadership*

67

Retain Your Employees

For a manager, it all comes down to keeping the people who keep your business in business. Is your culture one that turns people on and gets them excited about coming to work? Are all employees treated with dignity? Do their jobs have a meaningful purpose? That's important to retaining your best employees. It's only natural that people want to work and stay at a place that embraces caring and respect for others.

When you hire and invest in people, you create a valuable asset, and you want to hold on to them and keep them feeling motivated. So what have we found out about doing this? Research and surveys have proven time and again that it's not about the money, titles, or shareholder value. And let's face it: you may not have much power to control those aspects anyway. It all comes back to creating an environment where people want to work and will do just about anything to get hired and keep their jobs.

Managers who understand this work toward building a reputation in their organization that says, "Everyone wants to work here." The Men's Wearhouse is a good example of high employee retention. New hires spend about four days in one of the 30 sessions held yearly at the corporate university. The cost to the company? A cool million. The return on investment? Lower turnover than any of its competitors in the industry. And all managers know that the hiring process is complicated, time-consuming, and filled with uncertainty. Minimize having to do that by holding on to the people you have. Here are some additional pointers and ideas to remember for motivating and retaining your talent:

Know what keeps the people who keep you in business: It comes down to creating an environment where your employees feel right—a culture that suits them—like at Google, one of the Web's most successful and fastest-growing search engines. Here employees play roller hockey during work hours, bring their dogs to work, and eat lunch and dinner for free in the company café. The result? Employees work long, hard hours and love their jobs.

Understand the reasons employees stay: It's not about the money. Top performers want to work in a pleasant and progressive environment where they feel valued and respected. Money is secondary.

Let values and attitude be your guide: What people know is far less important than what they are. Organizations like Nordstrom, Rosenbluth International, Nucor Steel, and JetBlue believe that a truly successful organization is based on finding people with the right mind-set, values, and attitude, not simply experience. Hiring people whom you *want* to keep is an important step in building a culture that makes people want to stay with you.

"Recruit your people every day, even though your crew is already on board."
—Mike Abrashoff

PART 4

DEALING WITH DIFFICULT PEOPLE

Difficult people: they're those people you can't stand and who don't do what you want them to do or who do what you don't want them to do—and you don't know what to do about them!

Good news: you don't have to be their victim anymore. And while you can't change difficult people, you can communicate with them in such a way that they change themselves.

Your ability to recognize the four key behavioral intentions is the first step toward success in influencing people to change their behavior toward the positive.

With effective listening skills and speaking skills in your repertoire, you'll have the building blocks for specific strategies for the toughest behaviors. And as you make these positive communication skills a habit, you will be able to prevent many of the difficult behaviors from ever occurring.

There are difficult people and everyone has to deal with them: We identify 10 general types of troublesome behavior. You may have your own "least favorites."

There are effective ways to deal with these people: That's what this section is all about.

"This section will help you to identify and assemble elements of effective communication. You can get through and be one of the few who bring out the best in most people at their worst."

68

Recognize the 10 Most Unwanted Behaviors

What are the 10 most unwanted behaviors? We all answer this question slightly differently, depending on our own interpersonal strengths and weaknesses. But we would generally agree about which people are difficult and what they do that makes them difficult. This section identifies 10 specific behavior patterns that sane people resort to when they feel threatened or thwarted, that represent their struggle with (or withdrawal from) undesired circumstances.

- **The Tank:** Pushy and ruthless, loud and forceful, or with the quiet intensity and surgical precision of a laser, the Tank assumes that the end justifies the means. If you are in the way, you will be eliminated.
- **The Sniper:** This covert operator resents you for some reason. Instead of getting mad, he or she gets even by identifying your weaknesses and

using them against you, through sabotage, gossip, and putdowns.

- **The Know-It-All:** This person knows 98 percent of everything. (Just ask!) Know-It-Alls will tell you what they know—for hours at a time!—but won't take a moment to listen to your "clearly inferior ideas."

- **The Think-They-Know-It-All:** Although these people don't know that much, they don't let that get in the way. If you don't know much about what they're talking about, they may mislead you into trouble or throw a project off track.

- **The Grenade:** This person explodes in tantrums that seem disproportionate to the present circumstances, sending others ducking for cover and wondering what it's all about.

- **The Yes Person:** Quick to agree, slow to deliver, the Yes Person leaves a trail of unfulfilled commitments and broken promises. Although they please no one, Yes People overcommit to please.

- **The Maybe Person:** When faced with a crucial decision, the Maybe Person keeps putting it off until it's too late. Finally, there comes a point when the decision makes itself. Then it's nobody's default but his or her own.

- **The Nothing Person:** You can't know what's going on because the Nothing Person tells you nothing—no feedback, verbal or nonverbal.

- **The No Person:** This person says, "Every silver cloud has a dark lining" and "I'm not being negative; I'm being realistic." Doleful and discouraging, the No Person drives others to despair.

- **The Whiner:** These people wallow in their woe, whine incessantly, and drag others down with the weight of their generalizations that nothing is right, everything is wrong, and it's always going to be that way unless you do something.

Some initial ideas for dealing with the 10 most unwanted types:

Understand that everybody reacts differently to these types of behavior: The person who's most irritating to you may be perfectly acceptable to someone else.

Get to know these types: Each warrants a different response. Think about the people around you. Does anybody at work or at home fit one of these descriptions?

Recognize the part you play: We can all be difficult at times. Understanding these behaviors in yourself will help you in your success with others.

"There is a certain consensus in polite society about who difficult people are and what it is they do that others find difficult."

69

Choose Your Approach

Before we go any further, we need to stress the fact that there are at least four choices when dealing with people you can't stand. There's no magic formula; you are the best judge of which choice is right in any particular situation—although, as you'll see, we believe the first of these four choices is in fact a nonchoice.

The four choices are:

- **Stay and do nothing.** Doing nothing is not necessarily complete passivity; it may include both suffering and complaining to other people who can do nothing. Doing nothing is dangerous, because frustration with difficult people tends to build up and get worse over time. And complaining to people who can do nothing tends to lower morale and productivity, while postponing effective action.

- **Vote with your feet.** Sometimes, your best option is to walk away. Not all situations are resolv-

able, and some are just not worth resolving. Voting with your feet makes sense when it no longer makes any sense to continue to deal with the person. If the situation is deteriorating, if everything you say or do makes matters worse, and if you find yourself losing control, remember that discretion is the better part of valor. Then walk away. Like Eleanor Roosevelt said, "No one can make you feel inferior without your permission." Before you decide to walk, however, you may want to consider your two other choices.

- **Change your attitude.** Even if the difficult person continues to engage in the difficult behavior, you can learn to see the person differently, listen to the person differently, and feel differently about the person. There are attitudinal changes that you can make in yourself that will set you free from your reactions to problem people.

- **Change your behavior.** When you change the way you deal with difficult people, they have to learn new ways to deal with you. There are effective, learnable strategies for dealing with most problem behaviors. That's what this section is about.

To summarize:

Realize that difficult behaviors fit into types, but each situation is different: You need to decide what kind of response is called for in each situation.

Avoid trying to do nothing: That strategy is probably not sustainable. If the situation is bad enough, you'll probably have to act.

Change your attitude first, then your behavior: Sometimes an attitude change alone is enough. But it's *always* a prerequisite for the harder task of changing your behavior.

"Don't despair. Remember that when dealing with difficult people, you always have a choice. In fact, you have four choices."

70

Understand the Four Intents

The first step in changing your attitude toward the 10 most unwanted behaviors is to understand them. The key is the four intentions with which people respond to situations and in two variables: *assertiveness level* and *focus of attention*.

People range from passive (less assertive) to aggressive (more assertive). The assertiveness level is often influenced by the situation: during times of challenge, difficulty, or stress, people tend to move out of their normal "comfort zone" and become either more passive or more aggressive.

The focus of attention in a situation can be primarily on the task at hand—a *task* focus—or primarily on relationships—a *people* focus. In times of difficulty or stress, most people focus more on either the "what" (task) or the "who" (people) of the situation.

Now put the two variables together. A person can focus on *people* aggressively (e.g., belligerence),

assertively (e.g., involvement), or passively (e.g., submission) or on a *task* aggressively (e.g., bold determination), assertively (e.g., involvement), or passively (e.g., withdrawal).

We each have a comfort zone of normal—more or less acceptable—behavior that challenges, difficulty, or stress can cause us to leave for a zone of exaggerated—or problem—behavior.

Every behavior (whether acceptable or problem) has a primary intent or purpose that it's trying to accomplish. We've identified four general intents that determine how people will react in any situation:

- Get the task done.
- Get the task right.
- Get along with people.
- Get appreciation from people.

(These aren't the only intentions that motivate people, but they serve as a useful framework for understanding and dealing with difficult behaviors.)

When these intents become thwarted or frustrated, trouble arises. Behaviors can be pushed to the extreme—which may lead to the difficult behaviors outlined earlier.

The following diagram shows how the four intents relate to the four behaviors.

Task Focus

Intent:
Get it right

Intent:
Get it done

Passive ◄ **Normal Zone** ► Aggressive

Intent:
Get along

Intent:
Get appreciated

People Focus

Intents are constantly shifting, depending on the person and situation, which brings changes in behavior. So you should:

Understand the four intents: They all have their time and place in our lives. When we keep them in balance, the result is often more success and less stress.

Be attentive to communication patterns (words, tone, and body language): They reveal the primary intent of difficult people and indicate how to deal with them.

Don't be difficult: When your intents are thwarted, you may become a difficult person. The more you know about why people behave as they do, the more you can change yourself.

"Have you ever been astonished at how quickly a person's behavior can change from one moment to the next?"

71

Understand the First Intent: Get It Done

Have you ever needed to get something done, finished, and behind you? When you need to get it *done*, you focus on the task at hand. And when you *really* need to get it done, you speed things up, focus on action, and assert yourself. You may even become careless and aggressive, leaping before you look or speaking without thinking. The people around you become peripheral.

When this attempt to get things done is frustrated, it can distort the person's perceptions of a given situation. Suddenly, others appear to be wasting time, going off on tangents, or just plain taking too long. *The intent increases in intensity, and the subsequent behavior becomes more controlling.*

The three most difficult controlling behaviors are found in the Tank, the Sniper, and the Know-It-All.

- **The Tank.** On a mission to get things done, the Tank is unable to slow down and may push you around or run right over you in the process. The Tank has no inhibitions about ripping you apart personally, yet it's nothing personal: you just happened to get in the way. In an effort to control the process and accomplish the mission, Tank behavior ranges from mild pushiness to outright aggression.

- **The Sniper.** When things aren't getting done to his or her satisfaction, the Sniper attempts to control you through embarrassment and humiliation. Most people live in fear of public embarrassment—a fact that Snipers use to their advantage, by making loaded statements and sarcastic comments at times when you are most vulnerable.

- **The Know-It-All.** The Know-It-All controls people and events by dominating the conversation with lengthy, imperious arguments and eliminates opposition by finding flaws and weaknesses to discredit other points of view. Because Know-It-Alls are actually knowledgeable and competent, most people are quickly worn down by their strategy and finally just give up.

Intents shift over time. You may begin a task with the intent of getting it right, then find that you're running out of time and have to shift to getting it done. When starting a new job, you may lean

more toward getting along, but over time you may come to focus more on getting appreciation.

The key points:

Understand that behaviors are sometimes driven by the intent to get it done: This isn't necessarily bad or inappropriate. In fact, it may be needed.

Know the dynamics of the intent to get it done: It causes people to focus on the task, to speed up, to assert themselves. They may become careless, treat other people as peripheral, and act aggressively.

Recognize that the intent to get it done can lead to controlling behaviors: These can express themselves as the bullying of the Tank, the lethal comments of the Sniper, or the dominating lectures of the Know-It-All. But what they all have in common is they seek to take charge of you and the situation.

"If you need to get it done, you focus on the task at hand. Any awareness of people is peripheral or unnecessary to accomplishing the task. . . . You tend to speed up . . . , to act . . . , to assert. . . . You may even become careless and aggressive."

72

Understand the Second Intent: Get It Right

Getting it right is another task-focused intent that influences behavior. Have you ever sought to avoid a mistake by doing everything possible to prevent it from happening? When getting it right is your highest priority, you slow things down enough to see the details. You probably take a good, long look before leaping—if you ever leap at all. You may avoid taking any action because you feel unsure about what might happen as a result.

When the intent to get it right becomes thwarted or threatened, everything around this person begins to seem haphazard and careless. To add insult to injury, people seem to address these concerns with increasingly fuzzy terms.

When sufficient intensity is reached, the result is increasingly pessimistic and perfectionist behavior. The Whiner, the No Person, and the Nothing Person all exemplify this behavior.

- **The Whiner.** In our imperfect world, the Whiner believes that he or she is powerless to create change. Burdened and overwhelmed by all the uncertainty around what can go wrong, Whiners abandon all thought of solutions. Instead, as the feeling of hopelessness increases, they focus on any problems that can be used as evidence for their massive generalization. They begin to whine, "Nothing is right. Everything is wrong." This, of course, serves only to drive everybody else crazy— and the deteriorating situation provokes further whining.

- **The No Person.** Unlike the Whiner, the No Person does not feel helpless in the face of things going wrong. Instead, the No Person becomes hopeless. Certain that what is wrong will never be set right, No People have no inhibition about letting others know how they feel. "Forget it; we tried that. It didn't work then, it won't work now, and you're kidding yourself if anyone tells you different. Give up and save yourself from wasted effort on a lost cause." This attitudinal black hole pulls others into the No Person's personal pit of despair.

- **The Nothing Person.** When events fail to measure up to the standard of perfection, some people get so totally frustrated that they withdraw completely. This may be for failing to get it right: "Fine! Do it your way. Don't come crying to me if it does-

n't work out!" From that point on, they say—and do—nothing.

The key points:

Understand that behaviors are sometimes driven by the intent to get it right: Again, this isn't necessarily bad or inappropriate. In fact, it may be exactly what the situation calls for.

Know the dynamics of the intent to get it right: People concentrate on avoiding mistakes and slow down to pay more attention to all of the details. They may not take action because of concerns about the consequences. They may find fault with others for not caring enough.

Recognize that the intent to get it right can lead to perfectionist behaviors: This can express itself as the whining of the Whiner, the negativity of the No Person, or the silent withdrawal of the Nothing Person. But what they all have in common is their sureness that nothing works out positively.

"When getting it right is your highest priority, you will likely slow things down enough to see the details. . . . You may even refuse to take action because of a particular doubt about the consequences."

73

Understand the Third Intent: Get Along

A third intent is to get along with other people. This is necessary if you want to create and develop relationships. When there are people with whom you want to get along, you may be less assertive as you consider their needs and interests above your own. In other words, personal desires are of lesser importance than the intent to get along with another person.

The problem is that when people who are focused on getting along with others are uncertain about how others feel about them, they tend to take reactions, comments, and facial expressions personally. *Behavior becomes increasingly geared toward gaining approval and avoiding disapproval.* The three most difficult approval-seeking behaviors are the passive Nothing Person, the wishy-washy Yes Person, and the indecisive Maybe Person.

- **The Nothing Person.** Timid, uncomfortable, and uncertain, *get-along* Nothing People excel at

tongue biting. Since they don't have anything nice to say, they don't say anything at all. At their worst, they say nothing almost all the time. This, in many ways, is the perfect strategy to avoid conflict, to avoid hurting someone else's feelings, and to keep from angering anyone. However, since a Nothing Person can't relate authentically or speak honestly, he or she doesn't really get along with anyone.

- **The Yes Person.** Yes People attempt to get along with others by trying to please everyone. A Yes Person agrees to every request, without considering the consequences. Before long, the Yes Person has overpromised and underdelivered to such an extent that the very people he or she wanted to get along with are furious. In the rare instance where the promises are kept, the Yes Person's life is no longer his or her own, because all choices are made around other people's demands. This produces a deep-seated anxiety and much resentment in the Yes Person and can even lead to unconscious acts of sabotage.

- **The Maybe Person.** The Maybe Person avoids disapproval by avoiding decisions. After all, the wrong choice might upset someone, and who would be blamed? The solution is to put the decision off, waffle, and hedge until someone else makes the decision—or the decision makes itself. Like all the other difficult behaviors, this behavior perpetuates the problem it's intended to solve,

mainly by causing so much frustration and annoyance that the Maybe Person is locked out of meaningful relationships with others.

The key points:

Understand that behaviors are sometimes driven by the intent to get along: As we will see in subsequent lessons, establishing common ground is a good technique. But basing your actions—and your self-esteem—on your perceptions of how others see you is usually counterproductive.

Know the dynamics of the intent to get along: People tend to feel unsure about how others feel about them, so they take reactions, comments, and facial expressions personally and behave in ways that they believe will gain approval or at least avoid disapproval.

Recognize that the intent to get along can lead to approval-seeking behaviors: This can express itself as the withdrawn Nothing Person, the agreeable Yes Person, and the indecisive Maybe Person. But what they all have in common is you really don't know where they stand.

"If getting along is your top priority . . . , personal desires are less important than the intent to get along with another person."

74

Understand the Fourth Intent: Get Appreciated

This fourth intent requires a higher level of assertiveness, as well as a people focus, in order to be seen, heard, and recognized. The desire to contribute to others and *be appreciated for it* is one of the most powerful motivators. Studies show that people who love their jobs—as well as husbands and wives who are happily married—feel appreciated for who they are and what they do.

When the intent to get appreciated becomes distorted, the lack of positive feedback combines in a person's mind with the reactions, comments, and facial expressions of others and the person tends to take it personally. The intent to get appreciation intensifies in direct proportion to the lack of appreciative feedback, and the problem behavior becomes *increasingly aimed at getting attention*.

The three most difficult attention-getting behaviors that result from the desire to get appreciation

are the Grenade, the Sniper, and the Think-They-Know-It-All.

- **The Grenade.** Grenades feel they don't get any appreciation or respect. When the silence becomes deafening, look out for the Grenade's grown-up temper tantrum: "Nobody around here cares! That's the problem with the world today. I don't know why I even bother!" (While the Tank uses focused fire in a single direction, based on a specific charge, the Grenade produces out-of-control explosions in any and every direction: his or her outbursts may be completely unrelated to present circumstances.) Since this desperate behavior produces negative attention and disgust, the Grenade is even more likely to blow up at the next provocation.

- **The friendly Sniper.** This Sniper, a variation on the unfriendly sniper who's trying to undermine your self-control, actually likes you, and his or her sniping is a "fun" way of getting attention. Many people have relationships that include friendly sniping. Normally, the best defense is a good offense, because instead of offending, a return snipe is a sign of appreciation. But if the person on the receiving end doesn't give or receive appreciation in this manner, he or she may be laughing on the outside and hurting on the inside.

- **The Think-They-Know-It-All.** The Think-They-Know-It-All is a specialist in exaggeration, half-

truths, jargon, useless advice, and unsolicited opinions. Charismatic and enthusiastic, this desperate-for-attention person can persuade and mislead an entire group of naive people into serious difficulties. If you argue with the Think-They-Know-It-Alls, they turn up the volume and dig in their heels, then refuse to back down until you look as foolish as they do.

The key points:

Understand that behaviors are sometimes driven by the intent to get appreciated: We all want to be appreciated. It's how we get there that counts.

Know the dynamics of the intent to get appreciated: People who become more concerned about receiving positive attention can take lack of affirmative feedback personally and read too much into reactions, comments, and facial expressions.

Recognize that the intent to get appreciated can lead to attention-seeking behaviors: This response can express itself as the tantrums of the Grenade, the barbed jokes of the friendly Sniper, or the boastfulness of the Think-They-Know-It-All. But what they all have in common is they force you to notice them.

"The desire to contribute to others and be appreciated for it is one of the most powerful motivational forces known."

75

Recognize the Results of Threatened Intents

The four intents—get it done, get it right, get along, and get appreciated—have their time and place in our lives. The priority of those intents can shift from moment to moment. We normally balance them, for more success and less stress.

But what happens when a person's intent is not met? Let's look at each of the four intents and the results when those intents are threatened (see diagram).

- When people want to *get it done* and fear that it's not getting done, their behavior becomes more *controlling*. They try to take over and push ahead.

- When people want to *get it right* and fear that it will be done wrong, their behavior becomes more *perfectionistic*. They find every flaw and potential error.

- When people want to *get along* and fear that they will be left out, their behavior becomes more

approval seeking. They begin sacrificing their personal needs to please others.

■ When people want to *get appreciated* and fear they're failing at that intent, their behavior becomes more *attention getting*. They become difficult to ignore.

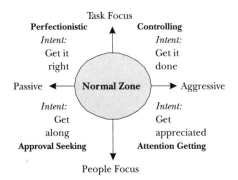

And so it begins: a person who might otherwise be inclined to act within the "normal zone" of human interaction starts drifting outside that zone, into a "gray zone" of less acceptable behavior and even into problem behavior.

The key points:

Understand that each of the four intents grows out of human nature: People are only human, after all!

Know that each intent leads to predictable kinds of behaviors: People who want to *get it done* become more *controlling*. People who want to *get it right* become more *perfectionistic*. People who want to

get along become more *approval seeking*. People who want to *get appreciated* become more *attention getting*.

Be alert to signs that someone's behavior is going beyond the "normal zone": That's when people who are acting acceptably start to become the people you can't stand.

"Once people determine that what they want is not happening, or that what they don't want is happening, their behavior becomes more extreme and therefore less tolerable to others."

76

Reduce the Differences

What makes some people so easy to relate to and others so difficult? We argue that conflict in a relationship occurs when the emphasis is on the *differences*, rather than on the *similarities*. Think of it as "United we stand, divided we can't stand each other."

So *reducing differences* is essential to dealing with people you can't stand. Success in communication depends on finding common ground and then trying to redirect the interaction toward a new outcome.

Two essential communication skills will help you reduce differences: *blending* and *redirecting*. "Blending" refers to behavior by which you reduce the differences between yourself and another person. "Redirecting" is any behavior by which you use a growing rapport to change the trajectory of your interactions. These skills are not new, of course;

they are part of normal human contact. In fact, you already use them, to some extent.

You can (and probably *do*) blend with people in many ways. Visually, you may blend by altering your facial expression, degree of animation, and body posture to match the other person. Verbally, blending occurs when you try to match the volume and speed of your counterpart's speech. And you blend conceptually with your words. When people feel like you've listened to them and you understand them, that's the result of blending. It's natural to blend with people whom you like or with people with whom you share an objective. Conversely, it's equally natural *not to blend* with people whom you perceive as difficult. But the failure to blend has serious consequences, because without blending, the differences between you become the basis for conflict.

Three key points:

Remember that no one cooperates with anyone who seems to be against him or her: In human relations, there's no middle ground. Unconsciously or consciously, people want to know, "Are you with me or against me?" You come across as either hot or cold in the relationship—perceived as being on common ground or as worlds apart.

Reduce the differences between yourself and the other person: You can blend by modifying your facial

expression, your gestures, your posture, the volume and speed of your speech, and your words.

Blend before you redirect, whether you're listening to understand or speaking to be understood: Only after establishing some rapport with your difficult person through blending will you be able to redirect the interaction and change the trajectory toward a worthwhile outcome. In dealing with a particularly difficult person, try to recall instances in which you have successfully blended with or redirected this person in the past and try to imagine circumstances in which you might do so again.

"Conflict occurs when the emphasis is on differences. Reducing differences can turn conflict into cooperation."

77

Listen to Understand

When people express themselves verbally, they generally want evidence of at least two things: they've been heard and they've been understood. A good communicator tries first to be a good listener. We advocate five steps toward good listening.

The first step toward good listening—introduced in the last lesson—is *blending*. How does someone know that you're listening and understanding? In essence, it's through the way you look and sound while the person is talking. Rather than distracting a difficult person with puzzled looks, interruptions, or statements of disagreements, help him or her to fully express his or her thoughts and feelings. You do this by nodding your head in agreement, making occasional sounds of understanding. Everything about you, from body posture to voice volume, must give the impression that you hear and understand.

When your problem person begins to repeat what's already been said, it's a signal to move to step

two: *backtracking*. This involves repeating back some of the actual words that another person is using, sending a clear signal that you're listening and that you think what the other person is saying is important. Translating or rephrasing what people have said is counterproductive and may create the impression that you haven't understood what's been said.

Having heard what the difficult person has to say, the next step is *clarifying*. At this point, you start to gather information about the meaning of what is being communicated. Ask some open-ended questions, which will allow you to figure out why the person is being difficult and what intent he or she is hoping to satisfy with that behavior.

It isn't always possible to understand why someone is upset. Emotions so cloud the reasoning capabilities of many people that their intelligence effectively becomes disconnected from their feelings. While it's virtually impossible to reason with an emotional person, it's still possible to look and sound like you understand, backtrack what you've heard, and then become curious enough to ask questions.

The fourth step is to *summarize* what you've heard. This allows you to make sure that both you and your difficult person are on the same page. When you do this, two things happen. First, if you've missed something, he or she can fill in the details. Second, you've demonstrated, yet again,

that you're making a serious effort to fully understand. This increases the likelihood of gaining cooperation from that person down the line.

Having listened carefully, you've now arrived at a crucial juncture. But before you move on, *confirm* with the person that he or she feels satisfied that his or her problem has been fully voiced. Ask if he or she feels understood. Ask if there's anything else that needs to be put on the table.

When enough sincere listening, questioning, caring, and remembering are brought together, understanding is usually achieved and a difficult person becomes less difficult and more cooperative.

The key points:

Listen first, listen well: You aren't likely to be heard (or understood) until the person has said what he or she has to say.

Learn and practice the five steps to good listening: Blend, backtrack, clarify, summarize, and confirm.

Make sure the other person knows you've heard and understood: You must establish this fact before you attempt to get him or her to hear and understand you.

"When two or more people want to be heard and no one is willing to listen, an argument is inevitable. Listen and understand first, and you unlock the doors to people's minds."

78

Reach a Deeper Understanding

We've discussed listening as a method for increasing trust, cooperation, and understanding. Yet sometimes the most important and useful aspects of communication are hidden—not just from the listener, but also from the speaker. When you identify the elements driving the difficult person, you reach a deeper understanding of that person's needs and intent.

Identifying the intent is an important first step to understanding your difficult person. You can apply the blending strategy to the four intents to increase cooperation and decrease misunderstanding.

For example:

- If you're dealing with someone whose top priority appears to be to *get it done*, your communications with him or her should be brief and to the point.

- If you're dealing with someone whose top priority appears to be to *get it right*, you should pay great

attention to the details in your communications.

- If you're dealing with someone whose top priority appears to be to *get along* with you, use considerate communications to demonstrate your interest in him or her.

- If you're dealing with someone whose top priority appears to be to *get appreciated*, recognize his or her contributions with words of enthusiastic appreciation.

In other words, it's crucial to ask yourself which intent lies behind a person's behavior or communication. Here's a surprise: *even if you're not totally sure what the key intent is, make the likely choice and act appropriately*. Because these intents are within you, in most cases your intuition will be right and you'll get a good response and increase rapport. And if it is not, then simply try something different.

Another way to reach a deeper understanding of your problem people is to *identify the criteria that are important to them*. Criteria are the filters on our points of view—the standards by which we measure ideas and experiences to determine if they're good or bad. Criteria become especially important when differing ideas or points of view are being discussed. Any time you identify criteria in a discussion, you generate more flexibility and cooperation.

Whenever a discussion starts to degenerate into conflict, try to ascertain the reasons why people are

for or against something. Then look for an idea or solution to the problem that blends those criteria together. That's another way to turn conflict into cooperation.

The key points:

Identify and act on intents: If, for example, someone appears to need your appreciation, make your appreciation clear.

Act on intent even when you're not sure of intent: Because these intents are within you, let your intuition guide you. And if what you're doing isn't working, then simply do something else.

Use criteria to reach a deeper understanding: What are the filters that your difficult person is using? How can you use your understanding of those filters to create new options?

"This . . . is about . . . the kind of understanding that will help you communicate effectively, prevent future conflict, and resolve current conflict before it gets out of hand . . . , the kind of understanding that results when you . . . closely examine the difficult behavior until you can see the motive behind it."

79

Speak to Be Understood

We've advocated effective listening as the best way to increase trust, cooperation, and understanding—and as a prerequisite for effective communication back to your difficult person. When you express yourself, it's important to do so in ways that produce positive effects. The signals, symbols, and suggestions that constitute our communication output provide a profound opportunity to influence relationships for the better. Here are five effective techniques.

■ **Monitor your tone of voice.** Your tone sends people either a positive or a negative message. Even when you choose your words well, if your tone of voice is hurried, hostile, or defensive, people may hear something very different from what you intended.

Mixed messages, caused by voice tones that don't match spoken words, cause miscommunications. If you hear yourself sending a mixed mes-

sage, call attention to it and explain what you're really saying: "I know I sound angry, but that is because this issue is so important to me."

■ **State your key intent.** Articulating your key intent lets people know where you're coming from. When your key intent is implied rather than stated clearly, misunderstanding can result. Telling people why you're telling them something before you actually tell them is a simple way to direct attention where you want it to go.

■ **Tactfully interrupt.** There are occasions when it is necessary to interrupt a difficult person. If someone is yelling at you, dominating a meeting, or complaining in endless cycles of negativity, an interruption may be an elegant solution. Done carefully, it can also be tactful.

A tactful interruption is done without anger, without blame, and without fear. Just say the difficult person's name over and over, in a matter-of-fact way, until you get his or her attention. These repetitions create an irresistible force that so distracts Tanks, Know-It-Alls, Grenades, or Whiners that they must stop talking to find out what you want.

■ **Tell your truth.** Honesty can be effective, no matter what difficult behavior a person engages in, if you're honest in a way that builds someone up rather than tears him or her down. Remember to tell the person why you are telling your truth before you actually tell it. State your positive intent

and why you think it's in the person's interest to hear what you have to say. Be sure to point out that it's *your opinion*. Then be specific about the problem behavior, show how the behavior defeats his or her intent, and suggest new behaviors to replace the old ones.

- **Stay flexible.** If your problem person becomes defensive, be willing to temporarily drop what you're saying to focus on his or her reaction. Do your best to fully understand any objections by backtracking, clarifying, summarizing, and confirming. This may seem time-consuming, but overall, it takes less energy than an adversarial conversation that goes nowhere.

The key points:

Once you have listened well, move on to effective speaking: One grows naturally out of the other.

Learn and practice the five techniques of speaking to be understood: Yes, effective speaking is harder and often takes longer—in the short run. But it's the best way to better outcomes in the long run.

Remember that "communicate" has the same origins as "common": To communicate is to establish a common understanding.

"What you say to people can produce defensiveness or trust, increase resistance or cooperation, promote conflict or understanding."

80

Project and Expect
the Best

The difficult behavior of problem people is often reinforced, and even escalated, by thoughtless and/or negative reactions from people around them. So if you want to have a positive influence, thoughtful responses are required.

It's in your interest to give difficult people the benefit of the doubt. It's also in your interest to help them break their reliance on negative behaviors and reinforce more constructive behaviors. If you do this habitually, a difficult person may come to see you as an ally rather than an enemy and be all the more ready to fulfill your positive expectations.

The power of expectations can't be underestimated. We call this phenomenon *Pygmalion Power*. If you tell people you have high expectations of them, they will not deny it. They will in fact take a step in that direction. But conversely, if you let it be known that you have low expectations, these will most likely be fulfilled, as well.

When your problem person is engaging in negative behavior, you may be tempted to say, "That's the problem with you. You always . . ." To use Pygmalion Power effectively, learn to say, "That's not like you! You're capable of . . ." and then describe how you want the person to be, as if he or she already were. And whenever your difficult person behaves well, reinforce the behavior by learning to say, "That's one of the things I like about you. You're always . . ." and then say what the person has done successfully so he or she will do it again.

Pygmalion Power is not the easiest technique to employ when someone is acting badly. You may have to spend some time mentally rehearsing it before you're able to talk this way with ease. You may have to force yourself to hope that the person can change, when all evidence is to the contrary. Yet, we have no doubt that you can surprise yourself delightfully with your power to bring out the best in people at their worst.

The key points:

Understand and embrace Pygmalion Power: Human nature is what it is. When you tell people that they're doing something wrong, they're very likely to get defensive. You can minimize that reaction by giving them the benefit of the doubt and expecting the best. Sometimes you get it!

Appreciate criticism: This is nothing more than the flip side of Pygmalion Power. If you tend to get defensive to criticism, perhaps you've noticed that it usually makes things worse. The implication is that your defenses are an admission of guilt, and anything you say may be used against you. Here's a simple way to rapidly shut down criticism without either internalizing it or fighting against it: verbally appreciate it. A simple "thanks for the feedback" may be all that it takes, and it's over. Alternatively, you can listen effectively, helping the critical person to be specific until you learn something useful, he or she learns it isn't about you, or he or she loses interest in criticizing you.

"It's a fact that people rise or fall to the level of your expectations and projections. Use projection strategies to motivate your problem people to change themselves."

81

Bring Out the Best in the Tank

When you're under attack by the Tank, you've been targeted as part of the problem. The aggressive behavior is meant to either shove you back on course or eliminate the obstacle that you represent. Your goal must be to command respect, because Tanks simply don't attack people they respect. Aggressive people require assertive reactions. Here's a five-step action plan that will send a clear signal that you are strong and capable.

- **Hold your ground.** Stay put. Don't change your position and don't go on either the offensive or the defensive. Wait until the attack is over, then tell the Tank what you're going to do about it (even if it means walking away)—and do it. Other times, you may need to proceed to the next step.

- **Interrupt the attack.** Say the person's name over and over until you have his or her full attention. Once you've begun this step, don't back off.

Aggressive people like assertive people who stand up for themselves, as long as this isn't perceived as an attack. Keep your voice volume at 75 percent of the Tank's volume. Then he or she will perceive you as assertive but not aggressive.

- **Backtrack.** Now that you have the Tank's attention, backtrack the main accusation. This sets a good example of listening with respect and conveys that you've heard him or her. A Tank has a short attention span. Two sentences will do. He or she will go back to venting. Wait a few seconds, then interrupt again and backtrack again.

- **Aim for the bottom line and fire!** Redirect the conversation to the bottom line—the Tank's if he or she is right, yours if he or she is wrong. The Tank wants to get it done, and your best chance of ending the attack is to blend with his or her intent. The bottom line varies with your situation but can usually be stated in about two sentences. Keep it short and sweet: the attention span of a Tank is extremely short. Try to establish that you and he or she are on the same side: e.g., "We both want what's best on this project." Or respond with a problem: e.g., "That's terrible; I'm here to help you and we're going to do something about it!" A take-charge attitude will definitely blend with a Tank. If you're not on the same side, just tell it like it is: e.g., "I'll discuss this with you when you're ready to communicate in a reasonable manner."

- **Peace with honor.** Never close the door in the Tank's face. When you leave the door open, the Tank has the opportunity to back off and probably will take it. You can let him or her have the last word . . . but you decide where and when this happens: e.g., "When you're ready to talk to me with respect, I'm willing to hear what you have to say."

There are three typical emotional responses to an attacking Tank. They're all natural—and all futile. So adjust your attitude:

Don't counterattack!: Avoid engaging with the Tank. You may win the battle, but you could still lose the war if the Tank decides to build an alliance against you.

Don't defend, explain, or justify: The Tank has no interest in your explanations, and defensive behavior is likely to further antagonize the Tank.

Don't shut down: Out of fear or to avoid conflict, you may be tempted to withdraw. But fear is a surefire sign to the Tank that the attack was justified and may inspire him or her to return for more.

"The Tank is confrontational, pointed, and angry, the ultimate in pushy and aggressive behavior."

82

Bring Out the Best in the Sniper

When events don't go as planned or are obstructed by others, a *get-it-done* person may try to eliminate the opposition through sniping. Your goal when dealing with the Sniper is to bring him or her out of hiding. Since the Sniper's limited power is derived from covert operations, rather than overt, once you've exposed a sniping position, that position becomes useless.

- **Stop, look, backtrack.** Since your goal is to bring the Sniper out of hiding, you must first zero in on his or her hiding place. If it seems that someone is taking shots at you, stop!—even in the middle of a sentence. Interrupting yourself brings attention to the Sniper, effectively blowing his or her cover. Look directly into the person's eyes for a moment, and then calmly backtrack his or her remark.

- **Use searchlight questions.** Now it's time to turn on the searchlight, asking a question to draw the

Sniper out and expose his or her behavior. The two best questions are based on intent and relevancy: "When you say that (backtrack), what are you really trying to say?" and "What does that (backtrack) have to do with this?" The key to asking a searchlight question is to keep your tone neutral and maintain a neutral (read "innocent") look on your face.

■ **Use Tank strategy if necessary.** If a Sniper becomes a Tank, you may have actually improved the situation; at least now you know what the problem is! Use the strategy recommended for dealing with the Tank not only to command respect from the Sniper but also to command respect from those who have witnessed the attack.

■ **Go on a grievance patrol.** If you suspect that someone is holding a grudge against you, but you're not certain, see what you can scout out. If you find evidence that someone is harboring a grudge, you may want to clear the air. If you're successful in bringing the grudge to the surface, listen carefully to all that your Sniper has to say. Once you fully understand the grievance, let your problem person know that you understand and express appreciation for his or her candid description of the problem.

■ **Suggest a civil future.** Whether in private or public, finish the interaction by suggesting an alternative behavior for the future. At the end of any

encounter with the Sniper, it's important to let him or her know that your preference in the future is open and friendly communication.

So . . .

Don't overreact: Reacting strongly to the Sniper may encourage him or her to dish out more of the same. The best attitude to develop is one of amused curiosity. Try not to take it personally; instead, focus on the Sniper, rather than yourself.

Distinguish between friendly Snipers and malicious Snipers: Friendly sniping has its origins in the intent to get appreciated, the need for attention. Malicious sniping, on the other hand, originates in the intent to get it done and fulfills the need for control by seeking to undermine the control of others.

For the friendly Sniper, try reframing: Take the remark as a sign of affection or a behavioral quirk. If you can't laugh at it, you can at least learn to laugh it off. Or just let the Sniper know you don't respond well to teasing or put-down humor. Since the person likes you, he or she may change his or her behavior around you. And when that happens, reinforce it by appreciating the person for the change.

"Whether through rude comments, biting sarcasm, or a well-timed roll of the eyes, making you look foolish is the Sniper's specialty."

83

Bring Out the Best in the Know-It-All

Know-It-Alls are knowledgeable and extremely competent people, highly assertive and outspoken in their viewpoints. Their intent is to get it done in the way that they have determined is best, so they can be very controlling, with a low tolerance for correction and contradiction. Know-It-Alls perceive new ideas as challenges to their authority and knowledge and will rise to those challenges. They will do anything to avoid humiliation.

Your goal with the Know-It-All is to open his or her mind to new information and ideas. But as we've seen, this isn't easy(!). With Know-It-Alls, it's next to impossible to get your two cents in.

- **Be prepared and know your stuff.** If there are any flaws in your thinking, Know-It-All radar will pick up on those shortcomings and use them to discredit your whole idea. In order to get a Know-It-All to consider your alternative, you must clearly

think through your information beforehand and be ready to present it clearly and concisely.

- **Backtrack respectfully.** Be forewarned: you'll have to do more backtracking with the Know-It-Alls than with any other difficult person. They must feel that you have thoroughly understood the brilliance of their point of view before you'll be able to redirect them to another point of view.

It's not enough to simply backtrack; your whole demeanor must be one of respect and sincerity. You want to look and sound as if the Know-It-All's view is in fact the correct one.

- **Blend with their doubts and desires.** If the Know-It-All really believes in an idea, it is because of specific criteria that make that idea important to him or her. You will find it helpful to blend with those criteria, if you know them, by acknowledging them before you present your idea. Then show how your idea takes those factors into account.

- **Present your views indirectly.** When the time has come to redirect the Know-It-All to your position, use softening words like "maybe," "perhaps," and "bear with me a moment" to sound hypothetical and indirect, rather than determined or challenging. Try questions rather than statements and "we" rather than "I."

- **Turn them into mentors.** By letting the Know-It-All know that you recognize an expert and are will-

ing to learn, you become less of a threat. This way, the Know-It-All spends more time *in*structing you than *ob*structing you. It is entirely possible that, with time, the Know-It-All will be more willing to listen to you, as well.

Adjust your attitude:

Don't use the Know-It-All's weapons: Resist the temptation of becoming a Know-It-All yourself. It will only serve to entrench the Know-It-All more firmly.

Don't resent the Know-It-All: It's not in the Know-It-All's nature to get a second opinion. Resentments will only lead to an argument, which is pointless.

Don't force your ideas on the Know-It-All: Train yourself to be flexible, patient, and very clever about how you present your ideas.

"Seldom in doubt, the Know-It-All has a low tolerance for correction and contradiction. If something goes wrong, however, the Know-It-All will speak with the same authority about who's to blame—you!"

84

Bring Out the Best in the Think-They-Know-It-All

People who behave like Think-They-Know-It-Alls are driven by the need to get appreciation. When they feel slighted in any way, they're likely to try harder than ever to attract attention. Think-They-Know-It-Alls push their way into conversations where they may not be wanted.

Your goal when dealing with Think-They-Know-It-Alls is to catch them in their act and give their bad ideas the hook. You'll be most successful if you can avoid putting the Think-They-Know-It-All on the defensive. Here's an action plan for bringing out the best in Think-They-Know-It-Alls.

- **Give them a little attention.** There are two ways to give a Think-They-Know-It-All attention. The first is to backtrack on his or her comments with enthusiasm. This lets the person know that you're paying attention (and it puts these types on the receiving end of their own foolishness). The

second way is to acknowledge the person's positive intent, without wasting your time on his or her information: you're giving positive attention without necessarily agreeing with his or her remarks.

- **Clarify for specifics.** If the person doesn't know what he or she is talking about and you do, this should be easy. Ask some revealing questions about the specifics of his or her information. Since Think-They-Know-It-Alls speak in huge generalizations, pay special attention to words like "everybody" and "always."

- **Tell it like it is.** Carefully redirect the conversation back to reality. Use "I" language to keep your remarks as nonthreatening as possible. To add irrefutable evidence, you can document your facts as you go.

- **Give them a break.** At this point, it has become clear that the Think-They-Know-It-All doesn't know what he or she is talking about and that you do. Resist the temptation to embarrass the person. Instead, give him or her a way out, minimizing the chance that the Think-They-Know-It-All will go on the defensive. Think-They-Know-It-Alls are not as attached to their ideas as Know-It-Alls. If you give them a way to go along with you, chances are they'll be ready to jump on your bandwagon.

- **Break the cycle.** Once people believe someone is just a Think-They-Know-It-All, they may stop giving that person any recognition at all, even when

he or she deserves it. But that increases the Think-They-Know-It-All's need for appreciation, so he or she engages in that behavior even more. "Break the cycle" means be ready to give credit where credit is due. Notice what this problem person is doing right and praise him or her for it. For some people, this attention will be all that's necessary to get the problem behavior to subside. With others, use a gentle confrontation to tell them the truth about the consequences of their negative behavior.

Adjust your attitude:

Don't burst their bubble: When you challenge Think-They-Know-It-Alls directly, their only way out is to counterattack with ever grander claims. And their conviction could sway others who don't know any better.

Don't be too quick to judge: We've all defended ideas that we didn't necessarily believe to be true.

"Think-They-Know-It-Alls can't fool all of the people all of the time, but they can fool some of the people enough of the time and enough of the people all of the time—all for the sake of getting some attention."

85

Bring Out the Best in the Grenade

When a person's efforts to get appreciation are thwarted by another's indifference, he or she may explode in a thinly disguised demand for attention. Losing emotional control is a defense strategy against the feeling of unimportance—a strategy frequently employed by the Grenade.

If, as an adult in a group, you've ever lost control of yourself, you know how humiliating this can be. Grenades hate themselves for their behavior—but this self-hatred often becomes the timing device that provokes the next explosion. This volatile cycle can continue unchecked, meaning that an ounce of prevention can be worth far more than a pound of cure! Here are the five steps to bringing out the best in the Grenade.

■ **Get the Grenade's attention.** This is the one time you may have to be louder than your problem person . . . but don't let it seem aggressive. Call his

or her name loudly, but in a tone of voice that's interested rather than angry.

- **Aim for the heart.** Show your genuine concern by telling your problem person what he or she needs to hear. By listening closely, you can determine the cause of the explosion, then backtrack while assuring the person of your concern. When you hit the heart, you'll be surprised at how quickly the Grenade cools down.

- **Reduce intensity.** When you see the Grenade responding, begin to reduce your voice volume and intensity. You can talk the person down from his or her peak of explosion to a normal level of communication by reducing the intensity level of your own communications.

- **Take time off for bad behavior.** There's no point in trying to have a reasonable conversation with your problem person while the adrenaline is still coursing. So take a little time out and let things cool the rest of the way down. Then ask to get back together to work things out.

- **Avoid setting off the Grenade.** This step addresses the long-term relationship and is, therefore, the most important in dealing with your problem person. Try to figure out what pulls the pin on your Grenade . . . and then don't pull it! If you discover that the pin puller is someone else in the office, training in interpersonal communication and conflict resolution might be helpful.

Adjust your attitude:

Release your anger: Adding your anger to an already volatile situation will simply be pouring gas on a raging fire.

Learn to look at the Grenade in a different way: Sometimes it can help to imagine the tantrum thrower as a two-year-old in diapers. Adjusting your perception of the Grenade will give you some much needed distance on the situation.

Listen to the Grenade: Whatever the cause of the explosions, if you're willing to invest a little time in actively listening to the problems the Grenade faces, you will slowly be able to reduce the frequency and intensity of the explosions.

"After a brief period of calm, the Grenade explodes into unfocused ranting and raving about things that have nothing to do with the present circumstances."

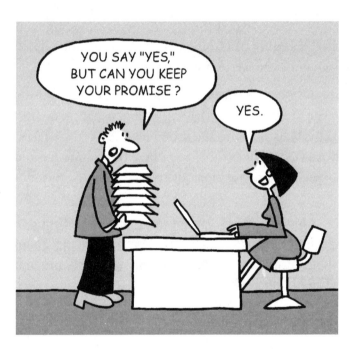

86

Bring Out the Best in the Yes Person

Yes People have a strong people focus and a weak task focus. They are extremely disorganized and frequently overcommit themselves as they try to run their lives based on the desires of other people. Sometimes they don't know how to follow through on something they've agreed to do; more often than not, they don't think about the consequences of what they're agreeing to do.

Yes People feel terrible when they can't deliver something they've promised. Yet they rarely feel responsible, because they can always find circumstances beyond their control that have caused the trouble.

Your goal with the Yes Person is to get commitments you can count on. Here are five steps to bringing out the best in the Yes Person.

■ **Make it safe to be honest.** Through nonverbal blending and verbal reassurance, make sure your communication environment is safe, so that you

and your Yes Person can honestly examine whether he or she will keep promises. As the person becomes more comfortable with you, his or her true thoughts and feelings will surface more easily.

- **Talk honestly.** If you think the Yes Person is angry or resentful about something or believes the excuses he or she is spinning, talk it out. Hear the person out without contradicting, jumping to conclusions, or taking offense. Acknowledge him or her for being honest.

- **Help them learn to plan.** Once you've listened to your Yes Person's point of view, it will be obvious to you why the person can't deliver on his or her commitments. This is the time to create a learning opportunity. Teaching your Yes Person simple task-management skills is a better use of your energy than getting upset at the person when he or she can't deliver!

- **Ensure commitment.** Thank your Yes Person for communicating openly with you and ask how he or she will approach the situation differently next time. In future projects, make sure the Yes Person is committed at the beginning. Have him or her summarize the project to demonstrate an understanding of what's involved. Write the commitment down. You may even come up with memorable deadlines to ensure that the time frame will stick. Finally, be sure to describe the negative consequences should your Yes Person fail to deliver.

- **Strengthen the relationship.** Look at every interaction as a chance to strengthen the relationship. Make an event out of every completed commitment and see mistakes and broken promises as an opportunity to help the Yes Person develop his or her skills.

Adjust your attitude:

Don't place blame: Blaming the Yes Person will simply make him or her ashamed; the behavior will continue as the person promises you anything he or she thinks will placate you.

Be patient: Recognize that your Yes Person lacks organizational skills and can't recognize or fix this without help. Once you've helped the Yes Person develop task skills, his or her helpful nature will make that person the best teammate you could want.

Help with task management: Ask the Yes Person to explain the basics of the project, the tasks involved, and any negative consequences if he or she doesn't meet the commitment. Then, help him or her plan toward the deadlines, to establish a time frame.

"To please people and avoid confrontations, Yes People say 'Yes' without thinking things through. They react to the latest demands on their time by forgetting prior commitments and overcommit until they have no time for themselves. Then they become resentful."

87

Bring Out the Best in the Maybe Person

Decisive people know that every decision has a downside and an upside and are able to weigh these possibilities as they make the best decision possible. Maybe People, by contrast, are unable to make decisions, especially when the consequences of their decisions could affect other people in a way that might lose them approval. So they put off the difficult decision, hoping that a better choice will come up. Unfortunately, with most decisions there comes a point when it's too late to choose: the decision just happens.

Maybe People have plenty of reasons for not getting help; they don't want to bother or upset anyone and they don't want to be the cause of anything's going wrong. Your goal when dealing with a Maybe Person is to give him or her a strategy for making decisions and the motivation to use it. Here are five steps to bring out the best in your Maybe Person.

- **Establish a comfort zone.** When you're dealing with people in the *get-along* quadrant, your best bet is to develop a comfort zone around the decision-making process. Take your time. Reassure the Maybe Person that you believe relationships are improved by open communication.

- **Surface conflicts and clarify options.** Patiently explore, from the Maybe Person's point of view, all of the options and obstacles involved in the decision. Listen for words of hesitation like "probably," "that could be," and "I think so" as signals to explore more deeply. If the person is worried about how you will feel should he or she decide something, provide reassurance that you will be fine and it won't adversely affect your relationship.

- **Use a decision-making process.** If you have a process that works well for you, teach it to your problem person. It could be as simple as listing with him or her all the pluses and minuses of each of the possibilities. Seeing these in a concrete form may make the strongest choice more obvious.

- **Reassure and follow through.** Once the decision has been made, reassure the Maybe Person that there are no perfect decisions and that his or her decision is a good one. Then *stay in touch* until the decision is implemented.

- **Strengthen the relationship.** Take a few moments from time to time to listen to the Maybe Person's concerns and help him or her learn the

decision-making process whenever the opportunity arises. With patient investment, the Maybe Person may become one of your most dependable decision makers.

Adjust your attitude:

Don't push the Maybe Person: Irritation, impatience, or anger will simply make the decision that much more difficult.

Be patient: If your Maybe Person feels pressured, he or she won't be able to relax and think clearly.

Stay calm: Intensity or intimidation will drive Maybe People deeper into their wishy-washy behavior. Even if you can force a decision, they will probably change their minds as soon as they're pressured by someone with a different agenda.

"In a moment of decision, the Maybe Person procrastinates in the hope that a better choice will present itself. Sadly, with most decisions, there comes a point when it is too little, too late, and the decision makes itself."

88

Bring Out the Best in the Nothing Person

Nothing People are passive, but they can be task-focused or people-focused depending on their intent—*get it right* or *get along*. When the intent to *get along* is threatened, shy people tend to withdraw and become ever more passive. When *get-it-right* Nothing People see their quest for perfection thwarted, they get frustrated and withdraw, convinced that nothing will change the situation, no matter what they say or do.

Although Nothing People seem to withdraw from conflict, inside they can be boiling cauldrons of hostility. Silence can be their form of aggression. Your goal with a Nothing Person is to break this silence and persuade him or her to talk. Here is a surefire five-step process to break your Nothing Person's silence.

- **Plan enough time.** Dealing successfully with a Nothing Person may take a long time. If you're

tense because of time constraints, you may be too intense to draw him or her out. The more intense you get, the deeper the Nothing Person withdraws into nothing. So pick the time and place for approaching your Nothing Person so that you have the time it takes.

- **Ask open-ended questions expectantly.** The best question for a Nothing Person is one that can't be answered with a yes, a no, or a grunt. Ask questions that begin with a "Who," "What," "When," "Where," or "How" to open up topics for discussion. Make sure that your nonverbal communication is also asking for a response. You must look and sound like you're about to get an answer. We call this the "expectant look"—and it *works*.

- **Lighten it up.** When nothing else is working, a little humor can go a long way. Making absurd, exaggerated, and impossible guesses as to the cause of the silence has cracked the armor of some of the most intransigent Nothing People.

- **Guess.** If your Nothing Person still isn't responding, try putting yourself in his or her shoes and thinking back over the course of events as to what that person might be feeling. Start talking out loud, rattling off possibilities whether they seem plausible or far out. It doesn't matter. If you can hit on or near the reason for the silence, the person will figure the jig is up and he or she might as well start talking. If you don't come close, the Nothing Per-

son may figure you don't have a clue and feel compelled to tell you what is going on.

- **Show the future.** Sometimes the only way to get Nothing People talking is to take them out of the moment and show them the consequences of their continued silence. Don't make idle threats, but be clear about how their behavior could damage the project or your relationship.

Adjust your attitude:

Slow down: The biggest challenge with a Nothing Person is to find the time to deal with him or her. To get something from a Nothing Person, you must be calm and relaxed.

Understand the intent: Nothing People can be task-focused, if their intent is to get it right, or people-focused, if their intent is to get along. Determine what matters.

Avoid getting angry: Your Nothing Person is trying to avoid conflict and disapproval. Getting angry will simply push a Nothing Person deeper into his or her nothingness.

"No verbal feedback, no nonverbal feedback. Nothing. What else could you expect from . . . the Nothing Person?"

89

Bring Out the Best in the No Person

The No Person is task-focused, motivated by the intent to get it right by avoiding mistakes. Perfection is his or her standard: when shortcomings get in the way, the No Person despairs and finds negatives in everyone and everything.

When you're dealing with a No Person, your task is to move from faultfinding toward problem solving. It may be impossible to stop the flood of negativity completely, but you may be able to turn the tide. Here are five steps to dealing successfully with a No Person.

- **Go with the flow.** The *worst thing* you can do with No People is to try to convince them that things aren't as bad as they think they are. The first step in dealing with No People is to allow them to be as negative as they want to be.
- **Use them as a resource.** No People can serve two valuable purposes in your life. First, they can be your personal character builders. If you want to

build strength, you lift heavy weights. If you want to build a positive attitude, spend some time being positive with a No Person. No People can also serve as an early warning system. Amid the negativity, there are often grains of truth. The No Person is sometimes aware of substantial problems that others have overlooked. We know of one company that has a No Person on its executive staff. By running every new plan by her, managers often find flaws that might otherwise have been overlooked.

- **Leave the door open.** No People tend to operate in a different time reality from other people. Any effort to rush them may actually slow them down. The wisest course of action with No People is to give them time to think, and leave the door open so that they can come back in when they're ready.

- **Go for the polarity response.** Sometimes, you can turn the tables on your No Person by suggesting the negative alternatives before he or she does. In such cases, No People may respond positively— either because they're convinced by your approach that you're dealing with the problem realistically or because they're so incurably negative that they want to prove you wrong even if they agree with you.

- **Acknowledge their good intent.** Assume good intent, and project that good intent onto negative behavior. For example, "Thanks for pointing out problems so we can all come up with solutions" or

"I appreciate that you want this to be right." Through Pygmalion Power, the No Person may come to believe it. This can lead the person to use his or her analytic perfectionism in a more constructive—and less difficult—way.

Adjust your attitude:

Maintain your perspective: There's usually some bad history involved when people behave negatively. You don't need to know what the circumstances are, but try to keep the No Person's actions in perspective.

Be patient: It may sometimes appear that changes take place at a snail's pace. But if you are patient, there are few things as gratifying as people's conquering their negative behavior.

Appreciate the No Person: He or she may bring up points worth considering, if you're wise enough to sort through the negativity. Just because the No Person goes to extremes doesn't mean that he or she is wrong.

"More deadly to morale than a speeding bullet, more powerful than hope, able to defeat big ideas with a single syllable. Disguised as a mild-mannered normal person, the No Person fights a never-ending battle for futility, hopelessness, and despair."

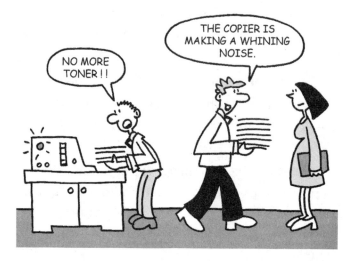

90

Bring Out the Best in the Whiner

While some complaining can be therapeutic for the complainer, and some can even be helpful to the listener, lots of complaining is simply wallowing. This is the Whiner's specialty. The Whiner's complaints have little to do with stress relief and are rarely helpful. Whiners are cousins to the No People, in the sense that their actions also emerge from the intent to get it right. But while they have a sense that things should be different, they have no idea how this should happen. So instead of taking action, they whine.

Your goal with Whiners is to form a problem-solving alliance. (And if this doesn't work, your revised goal is to get them to go away!) The best thing you can do for people who feel helpless when they encounter difficulty is to *diminish their helplessness*, by working with them to identify solutions.

Here are five action steps to work successfully with a Whiner.

- **Listen for the main points.** Listening to a Whiner complain is probably the last thing you want to do. But it's a crucial first step. You may even want to take notes. This proves to the Whiner that you're listening, and it will ensure that you recognize the complaint if the Whiner tries to recycle it.

- **Interrupt and get specific.** Take command of the conversation and ask clarification questions to get the specifics of the problem. If your Whiner isn't able to be specific, suggest that he or she go out and gather more information.

- **Shift the focus to solutions.** Because Whiners often complain in vague generalizations, they don't usually look at problems long enough to start thinking about solutions. Asking them what they want can start to move their minds in an entirely new direction.

- **Show them the future.** When people feel helpless, it's constructive to give them something to look forward to. Offer to set up a meeting with the person they're complaining about or simply set a time to discuss the problem further. You may find it helpful to suggest that they come back to you with possible solutions within a specific time frame.

- **Draw the line.** If the previous steps haven't produced a real change, it may become necessary to draw the line. If your Whiner begins the cycle of

complaints again, shut him or her down. Make it clear that talking about problems without solutions isn't a good use of your time . . . or anyone's.

Adjust your attitude:

Don't agree or disagree with Whiners: If you agree, it simply encourages them to keep whining. If you disagree, they may feel compelled to repeat their problems.

Don't try to solve Whiners' problems: You won't be able to solve their problems for them; you'll need their participation.

Don't ask Whiners why they're complaining: They'll simply see this as an invitation to start over from the beginning.

"Whiners feel helpless and overwhelmed by an unfair world. Their standard is perfection, and no one and nothing measures up to it. But misery loves company, so they bring their problems to you. Offering solutions makes you bad company, so their whining escalates."

91

Take Action Steps

The communication lessons in this section are not intended to be a quick fix, but a path to long-term solutions for problems in human relationships. The longer it takes for a problem to develop, the more time and energy you must invest in turning things around. As you begin to apply these attitudes and strategies, chances are that you will have some easy successes . . . and some unsuccessful efforts. More important than "winning" or "losing," though, is having more choices, opportunities, and alternatives to suffering. You can now empower yourself to be the cause of what happens next, rather than the victim of what others have done.

Difficult people are a part of every person's life. They've been here since the beginning of time—running away, blaming, withdrawing. But with commitment and perseverance, each of us can do our part to reduce misunderstandings and eliminate the conflicts that plague the earth. And without becom-

ing too grandiose, it's fair to say that the future of humanity depends on each of us *learning how to stand each other*, in spite of our differences.

Though you can't directly change anyone else, your flexibility and knowledge can help people to change themselves. So the next time you're dealing with someone you can't stand, remember this: Life is not a test; it's an actual emergency. Good luck!

Here are a few simple action steps you can take immediately:

- **Resolve to become an effective communicator.** Make it your goal to become an effective communicator; take advantage of all available opportunities to practice and perfect these techniques. Pay attention! Whether you're watching a movie or attending a meeting, you'll find lots of examples of people using or failing to use the skills and strategies in this section.

- **Find a communication partner.** Team up with communication partners who are as eager to learn as you are. Share resources (like this book) with your partners so that you'll have a common language in your discussions. Meet once a week to discuss what you've observed, learned, and tried during the preceding week. More than any other action you can take, regular meetings with communication partners can remind you to pay attention, while keeping you focused on developing and improving your skill.

- **Count your blessings!** If you have the luxury of reading this book, you're already better off than perhaps 80 percent of the earth's population. You probably have a roof over your head, sufficient food, people you care about, and some who care about you. Life is difficult enough without filling yourself with negativity and wasting your life force on worry and stress. If you remember to count your blessings today and every day, then you'll have the strength and focus to enjoy the challenges presented by difficult people.

"While you can't change difficult people, you can communicate with them in such a way that they change themselves. It's a matter of knowing how to get through to them when they're behaving badly."

PART 5

PLANNING AND EXECUTING STRATEGY

Every business leader would like to create a sound strategy and have it executed well. Accomplishing this, however, remains an elusive goal for most business organizations.

Devising and implementing new and innovative strategies to exploit opportunities in a competitive world is daunting. Clearly, no one strategy fits all companies.

As with most complex problems, the solution to planning and executing strategy lies in creating a practical, step-by-step methodology that breaks the problem into manageable components to be addressed in a logical sequence.

Virtually everyone in our society is touched by the strategic choices firms make about their products and services. These decisions affect the workers, customers, competitors, investors, and communities of today's businesses.

Strategy is often contrasted with tactics, another term with military origins. While strategy represents the big picture about "doing the right things," tactics are more about the details of "doing things right." Strategy sets the *direction* in which the organization will proceed, while tactics determine *how* it will proceed.

The major strategic challenges for firms encompass how to please customers, win orders, and simultaneously achieve financial objectives on an ongoing basis.

For example, a firm could have a strategy to build market share by selling the lowest-priced product in its market. After implementation of the strategy, the competitors will react, and the firm's strategy will need to adapt to meet the new challenges. There is no stopping point and no final battle. The competitive cycle continues on perpetually.

An organization's strategy should evolve over time as a blend of the intended strategy and the firm's responses to events, learning from experiences, and the emergence of new information and ideas. It is an iterative crafting process of making and implementing decisions, observing, analyzing, and learning from the results, and then making decisions anew.

To create, plan, and implement strategies, one should first learn to think in a way that combines

the rational and the intuitive in analyzing both hard and soft data to arrive at a unique interpretation of opportunities.

"Strategy is a process, not an event."

92

Manage Strategically

Many managers have a disdain for strategy and strategic planning, assuming that they are too theoretical for practical use. Every successful company, however, benefits from an effective strategy. The strategy might have been developed through formal analysis, trial and error, intuition, or just luck. Regardless of its origin, a strategy was indeed executed, whether managers were aware of it or not.

If a business has an excellent strategy and effective implementation, it will likely be successful. If a company has a poor strategy, however, it is probably going to fail in the long run. But what if a firm has a strength in strategy formulation *or* its ability to implement, but not both?

We know that some businesses have exceptional strategies and succeed in spite of mediocre operations. For others, it doesn't matter how well they make or deliver their product because nobody wants it. Great implementation simply cannot com-

pensate for a poor strategy. Having an effective strategy, though, is not necessarily more important than effective implementation. In the end, we must acknowledge that a company needs both to guarantee success.

Strategy is a long-term concept and, importantly, deals with change. The leader of a business, in seeking a prosperous future, must consider what might lie ahead and understand the driving forces of change and their likely impact on the business. Managers must determine which actions they should be taking now to prepare for what they expect in and desire for the future.

Tactics, in contrast, focus on the present. Tactics emphasize taking actions to execute the strategy, such as meeting demand, satisfying customer needs and desires, improving efficiency, and controlling quality and costs so as to make a profit and meet other short-term goals.

Evidence that a business's current strategies and operations have been effective includes current profitability and positive trends. Management must continually question whether these current strategies will continue to be successful in the future. Although some strategies last a long time, successful strategies do not last forever. Environments evolve, competition intensifies, and requirements for leadership talent shift. Strategies must transform in response.

To benefit from using the strategic management process to develop and implement strategies:

Use it to provide a framework: You can use the process to face and prepare for the future. This also requires attention to the present and the short-term horizon.

Let it guide you logically while requiring creativity: The process requires the team to generate ideas as well as consider the administrative details and functional activities that must be coordinated for successful strategy implementation.

Ensure widespread participation, which culminates in decisive plans: As a result, the process improves communication, motivation, and execution.

"Every activity should begin with a vision, purpose, goals, and objectives. These dreams are not likely to be realized without an effective strategy."

93

Follow the Logic

The strategic management process helps you first to understand your business's current situation and trends, next to determine a direction and desired state for the business, and finally to understand and identify what must be done to close the gap between the organization's current and desired positions.

Strategic management encompasses four tasks, each building on those that precede it:

- **Strategic learning** requires understanding the firm's operations and results. Learning also requires that you continually scan the environment and process the relevant information. The goal is to acquire a profound knowledge of the business and the environment in which it operates.

- **Strategic thinking** is a creative and analytic activity that builds on the knowledge developed

in the learning phase. Through the strategic thinking phase, you determine *what you want to do* in a strategic sense and the issues that must be addressed for success.

- **Strategic planning** has the aim of determining how best to *address strategic issues to achieve your strategic objectives.*

- **Strategic action** involves the *implementation* and *execution* of the strategic plans. Strategic action should involve activity at all levels of the organization.

A diligent completion of the tasks and a willingness to learn—to see things in new ways—are prerequisites for an effective strategic management process.

Strategic thinking requires creativity, which generates wide ranges of options to be considered. The more options you develop, the more likely you are to find the best one. Strategic thinking also encompasses a series of strategic choices that should be guided by the vision, mission, and values of the organization, including the following:

- What business do you want to be in?
- In what direction do you want to take the business?
- What are the goals of the business?
- How are you going to compete?

- What functional strategies do you need to be successful?

The functional strategies involve creating competencies throughout the organization to support the business strategy. The functions are generally considered to include marketing, production/operations, human resources, and finance. Detailed plans should be developed for various levels of the organization, all consistent with the articulated strategy.

Finally, the action phase of strategic management involves implementing the strategic plans. All members of the organization are involved in this phase of activity every day, whether mindful of it or not.

As you develop your strategic management skills:

Keep in mind that the strategic management process is deceptively simple: Learn, think, plan, and do. The devil is in the implementation.

Develop a profound knowledge of your business and its environment: These initial steps of the strategic management process build a foundation for the subsequent ones.

Assess constantly throughout the strategic management process: Continually review your implementation choices for consistency and fit.

"Continuous improvement is a requisite of competitiveness. Never let it rest."

94

Assess Your Company's Readiness

Is your business ready to take on the challenge of creating, planning, and implementing a strategy? You can determine your readiness by answering several questions. Think of this as a *readiness audit*.

Why are you thinking about strategy at this time? Is it for the right reasons?

Are you considering your strategy because, while moderately successful, you have a gnawing discomfort that things might be beginning to deteriorate? Or, do you aspire to move your business to the next level of size, profitability, or performance? Are you facing unprecedented competition?

Does your business have the right leaders?

Leadership plays a major role in both creating and executing strategy. In fact, organizations seldom advance beyond the capability of their leaders. It is important to determine whether leaders throughout the organization are able and willing to commit

to strategic management—especially those at the top.

The major distinction between day-to-day management and strategic leadership involves *perspective*.

Management focuses on the present, with emphasis on executing current strategies and meeting current performance objectives.

Strategic leadership focuses on the future, with emphasis on understanding the factors influencing the future, anticipating their likely impact on the business, setting longer-term goals, and developing strategies for achieving them.

Be certain your team has leadership capabilities for both activities.

Do you have a set of relevant guiding principles in place?

An organization should have a vision, a mission, and a set of core values that are relevant to its current situation and embraced by its leaders. The strategy and plans will be built upon these principles.

Are the right people in the right jobs?

The leader must get the right people in the right jobs and get rid of the wrong people. The right people solve problems and get things done without burdening management. The wrong people not only don't solve problems but also create additional problems and distractions.

Do any other current issues need to be addressed?

If a business has substantial internal or operational problems, lacks a viable business model, or is not adequately capitalized, the managers should address these issues before taking on strategic management.

Do the key managers understand the need to think more strategically? Are they personally committed to making the effort?

Understanding and commitment are necessary for success. Honest and realistic answers to the questions above will reveal whether your organization is ready to proceed.

To conduct your readiness audit, do the following:

Start by identifying the key leaders in the organization: Assess their willingness and capabilities to participate in a strategic management process.

Ensure that you have a relevant set of guiding principles: They will be the foundation of all strategic decisions going forward.

Identify any current issues, including personnel, that must be resolved: Attend to them before attempting any meaningful strategy work.

"You can prep for only so long; eventually you have to play the game."

95

Plan to Plan

You are now ready to begin the strategic planning process. It is important to find a logical starting point for the work, one that recognizes efforts that are already under way and issues that have already been resolved.

A key decision is the level of the effort to which your management team will commit. Not all situations require the same level of effort, nor are all teams capable of undertaking an extensive effort. Three levels of effort—*abbreviated*, *moderate*, and *extensive*—are described below.

In an *abbreviated* process, the CEO and other key executives typically carry out the strategic planning work, with the help of perhaps a few others, carefully selected. The process is essentially a series of meetings, with research and analytic tasks done by individuals or small teams. The outcomes should include a competitive strategy for the organization,

functional strategies, and action plans for critical issues and initiatives.

In a *moderate* process, the effort is expanded to include a few task forces, especially for conducting research and analyzing results. The task forces will include members from the functional areas likely to be affected by the strategic process. The outcomes of a moderate process should include those for the abbreviated process plus more thorough integration of the strategic goals into operating goals, budgets, and plans.

In an *extensive* process, the CEO often delegates the work to a steering committee, with a champion as chair. The champion should be a person who is respected throughout the organization, knows the business well, can think conceptually, has good people skills, and is well organized. Enthusiasm for the effort is important. The champion should report directly to the CEO for the process.

The steering committee under the champion should have a cross-functional and multilayered membership. In particular, the steering committee should establish the task forces and monitor their efforts to gather and analyze information and make recommendations. The steering committee should also develop a master work plan that delineates the schedules, responsibilities, and deliverables. Outcomes should mirror those for the moderate process with a totally integrated planning cycle.

Regardless of the complexity of your situation, the following three directions will help you start planning your approach to strategic management:

Select a logical starting point: It should build on what has previously been decided, as well as the company's agreed-upon current competitive position. Make sure all key objectives, goals, and assumptions are clear to all participants.

Determine the level of the effort required: The effort typically reflects the complexity of the situation. The process should be the simplest and least cumbersome for the circumstances.

Design an appropriate process: Outline plans to perform the work in a logical sequence. Avoid building elaborate systems that generate ponderous written documents and wear out the participants.

"Designing a process to fit the circumstances in a given situation is the foundation for a successful implementation of strategic management."

96

Define Your Businesses

To plan and implement strategy, you must first determine if you are in more than one business. Defining business segments is a cornerstone of the strategic management process. A company must develop, nurture, and implement basic strategies for each business in which it engages.

If your organization is a holding company with numerous business units, it is obvious that it has multiple businesses. A business unit or division is typically a semiautonomous or autonomous organization consisting of at least one independent business and possibly more. Holding company strategies address the appropriateness of the various business units (and potential acquisition targets) for inclusion in the corporate portfolio.

Segmenting your firm's activities into its distinct businesses will be complicated, however, when lines of business are integrated and share strategies or resources.

The following questions will help you identify which businesses are strategically separable:

■ Does the unit have a clear set of external customers? Are the majority of sales made outside the firm? An internal supplier may be an operating unit but not necessarily an independent business.

■ Does the unit have a group of external competitors?

■ Does management of this unit have discretion over the nature of products and services offered, and the authority to develop the recommended course of action regarding products and markets?

■ Does management of this unit have the authority to make crucial operating decisions, such as choosing suppliers and distribution channels?

■ Is it possible to measure the financial performance of this unit? A business unit must be a true profit center; its revenues and/or expenses (and hence profits) must not be the result of negotiations among organizations within the firm.

Operating units that do not satisfy most of the above criteria will probably have problems managing their own affairs and most often do not qualify as true businesses.

Consider the following three concepts when identifying a firm's businesses:

Apply the strategic management process at both the corporate and the business unit levels: At the corporate or holding company level, the task is one of portfolio management. What businesses do you want to be in or exit? How will you allocate resources? At the business level, competitive strategies are developed and implemented.

Recognize that business segmentation is key in the development of a strategic management process: It is at the business unit level that the most time and effort are required and where strategies that address issues such as product offerings and attributes, marketing decisions, and pricing are developed.

Prepare to address organizational structure often as you change your strategies: The structure of the organization must support your strategies. Do not ignore, however, the benefits to the organization of shared services and economies of scale and scope when making organizational adjustments.

"Strategies are formulated at the level of the business. Before you formulate strategies, you must first determine how many businesses you have."

97

Understand Your Model

A thorough understanding of your firm's business model is necessary for formulating and implementing strategy. The business model of an organization encompasses the realities that determine the profitability of the firm: volume and revenue, costs and profitability, and capitalization.

Volume is the driving force of a business model. Sales volume translates internally into the resources needed to deliver the expected amount of goods and services in a timely fashion.

Revenue is the result of volume and prices. Pricing strategies are generally among the most important decisions management makes, because they not only determine unit revenue but also impact the number of units sold and, hence, total revenue. Pricing is a crucial strategic decision.

Businesses have different economic characteristics determined by their expense structures. An understanding of the cost structure of your busi-

ness, particularly the distribution of fixed and variable costs, is essential. In general, businesses with high fixed costs must place special emphasis on achieving volume sales goals; those with low fixed costs should focus on price.

Businesses have different economic structures in terms of investment intensity, i.e., the quantity of assets required to support a dollar of sales. Process manufacturing businesses, such as paper mills or power generating stations, are very asset-intensive. Service businesses in general are less capital-intensive.

Determine what drives profitability. Which products are most important in generating profits? Which customers? How do you win these orders? How do you (or your competitors) create loyal customers? Which drives your profitability—volume or pricing?

Consider the return on investment (ROI), i.e., the relationship between profits and the investment required to generate them. The financial marketplace sets the desired ROI based on perceived risk. Examine benchmarks for appropriate measures of ROI, such as return on equity, return on net assets, and return on assets.

The final part of the business model is the decision on *how to fund the required investment.* Short-term borrowing can be used for temporary asset requirements such as seasonal inventories. Long-term requirements such as fixed assets should

be funded by long-term capital—either debt or equity. Internally generated funding is also a very attractive source of funds. Does your business model generate free cash flow?

Below are three tips for understanding your business model:

Do the analysis: Gather the data, take the time, and solicit the range of perspectives needed to guarantee a sound understanding of the business model.

Identify the key drivers of profitability: Examine products, customers, and fixed and variable costs. Do not overlook the relationships among your products; loss leaders might create opportunities for truly profitable accompanying sales.

Do not overlook funding and investment requirements: Owners, shareholders, and parent corporations expect a fair return on their investment. Inability to provide this return indicates a deficiency in the business model.

"The interfaces between marketing, manufacturing, and finance must provide for a profitable operation."

98

Know Your Market

One of the important challenges of strategy formulation and implementation is to thoroughly understand the markets you serve and the needs and desires of your customers. This understanding will be essential in developing your marketing strategy, which must match market preferences with existing and potential products or services.

Numerous *social and political factors* affect the attractiveness of the environment in which a business functions, including demographics and trends, laws and regulations, taxation and subsidies, power of special interest groups, unionization, and societal attitudes. The strategist must identify and take advantage of these macro trends.

Some industries are more attractive than others because of the *competitive dynamics of the players*. Michael Porter, of the Harvard Business School, has identified five forces that define industry competition:

- The threat of new entrants
- The power of buyers
- The power of suppliers
- The threat of substitutes
- The intensity of rivalry among existing competitors

Each of these forces asserts an influence on industry competitiveness and profitability.

The *market* in which a business operates may have characteristics that are somewhat different from the industry in general. The market is usually defined by some combination of type of customer, product or service, and/or geography. Important factors you will want to understand are:

- Market maturity, cyclicality, and/or seasonality
- Market size (dollars and units) and growth rate, by segment
- Market share distribution among competitors
- Market sensitivity to product offerings and price changes
- Switching costs of customers
- Pricing power

Financial characteristics are also an essential consideration when you're deciding on entering, remaining in, or leaving a business. Financial characteristics include profitability and margin structure, capital intensity, capacity utilization, and financial barriers to entry and exit.

Consider these three pointers when conducting your analyses and developing responses:

Don't fight the macro trends or industry forces: Instead, identify them and hitch a ride. Pursue strategies that position your company so it can take advantage of trends, best defend itself against industry forces, or influence the trends or forces in its favor.

Look for a growing market: Finding an attractive market that is growing and in which you have the skills and resources to compete will pay off in many ways. A growing market will allow firms to grow even while they lose market share, providing an opportunity for other firms to grow aggressively and capture share.

Critically assess the needs and desires of your customers—and potential customers: Assign creative and open people to this essential task and make sure it gets the attention it deserves. A cornerstone of strategy formulation is determining what customers really want and need—not just what you think they want and need.

"The business graveyard is full of firms that failed to understand their markets."

99

Assess the Terrain

Before devising strategies, you must understand the competitive landscape as it exists and as it is changing. You should examine and understand what competitors have done in the past, are doing now, and are likely to do in the future. The aim of this assessment is to find, for your firm going forward, a unique and defensible mix of product, marketing, and pricing strategies, given the direction your competitors will likely take.

This approach requires a thorough understanding of competitors' strengths and weaknesses, leadership, resources, and goals in order to estimate their possible approaches to competition. It is also useful to examine a benchmarking analysis comparing your organization's financial results with those of your competitors.

You must also examine forces driving change, which are related to but different from industry competitive forces. Driving forces create the oppor-

tunity for significant change at a particular point in time. An example of a driving force is the impact of the Internet on service firms.

While the environment is complex, most significant change is driven by only a few driving forces. You need to begin by identifying the primary forces and then understand their trends and potential impact on your industry, customers, and business.

Important activities involved in understanding driving forces of change include:

- *Identification*—Survey your firm's environment to detect changes already under way that might impact your business. Pay particular attention to technology, regulations, and the links in your supply chain.

- *Monitoring*—Once you've identified the driving forces, monitor them systematically.

- *Competitive intelligence*—Understand your rivals' strengths and weaknesses as well as how they might influence changes in the industry's competitive structure and, in particular, your relative position.

Remember: you are not really trying to predict the future, but to better understand possibilities and probabilities so that you can take an appropriate stance as you make your strategic decisions. An important caution is to recognize the degree of

uncertainty inherent in your situation and judiciously make accommodations for it.

Here are three tips to keep in mind as you search for competitive advantages and relevant driving forces:

Know your industry: If you don't get the facts, the facts will get you. Do not overestimate or underestimate your competitors; you cannot know them too well.

You can't exploit a force you don't understand or a trend you haven't identified: You are looking for relevant forces that are not under the control of your firm or industry but that can profoundly change the way business is conducted. Be vigilant.

Incorporate the driving forces into your strategies: Go forward; get started down the learning curve. If you don't, a competitor will.

"If you don't get the facts, the facts will get you."

100

Understand Opportunities and Threats

The purpose of most strategy implementation efforts is to exploit opportunities and/or to counter threats. You have the advantage of being able to select the opportunities to pursue. Threats, on the other hand, may be imposed on you.

Where should we look to identify opportunities and threats? Major sources include the industry (for substitute products or disruptive technologies), competitors (to assess their strengths and weaknesses), the general environment (for economic, social, political, or technological events and trends), and the organization's specific environment (for shifts in market characteristics). In particular, listen to your customers' feedback and questions.

It is usually better for your firm to be the first to acknowledge and exploit applicable new developments. A head start gives you the first-mover advantages of experience, scale, and recognition over later entrants. On the other hand, advantages some-

times accrue to followers, who learn through observation and typically invest far less than leaders.

You should *devise ways of exploiting identified opportunities*. What resources and competencies will be required? Are they available? If not, how might you get them? Is there a limited time window for the opportunity? What are the attendant risks? How do you minimize them? Are they risks that you can afford to take? Can you risk **not** acting?

You should also *consider creating additional opportunities through stretch objectives or breakthrough strategies*, by which you think the unthinkable and then work to bring about the desired results. Consider, for example, what it would take to ensure that you win all of your bids or capture all of the business of your largest customers. How can you get there or at least move in that direction?

Threats are external conditions in the firm's environment that carry potentially negative consequences. Examples of threats are changes in customers' needs or tastes, substitute products, inadequate supplies of skilled labor or raw materials, new government regulations, and potential litigation.

Threats must be evaluated continually. How likely are they to materialize? How soon? What is their potential impact if they do materialize? How can you reduce it? For which ones should you prepare immediately?

Here are three tips for managing your opportunities and threats:

Identify and exploit opportunities: That's the essence of success. Give widespread recognition to employees who find ways to innovate. Place bets on multiple new products and services; some will pay off handsomely, but be prepared to lose your total investment on products that fail.

Do not ignore threats: That attitude could lead to failure. Be attentive to identifying and monitoring potential threats to your business. A failure to do so could mean devastating results.

Take time to think the unthinkable about your company and its products: This exercise will stretch your thinking and help you uncover valuable opportunities.

"You cannot know too much about your customers or your competitors."

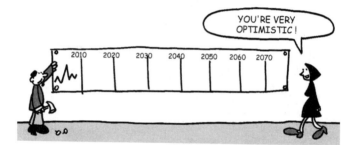

101

Set Feasible Goals

For nearly every business, the most important measures of corporate performance are the interrelated goals of return on investment (ROI); growth in revenues, earnings, or market share; and adequacy of cash flow to fund the growth.

The appropriateness of a company's goals can be measured by comparisons with the performance of companies in the same industry and, ultimately, the wider array of investment opportunities across the spectrum of all industries, as firms compete for investment capital.

In the matter of corporate goals and performance, it is essential that you choose a business in which to compete that offers a reasonable chance of meeting your financial goals and objectives.

The first element of strategy formulation is to select the business in which you will compete. If it is determined that entering into or continuing in an industry is likely to be successful, the strategist must

determine the direction the business will take (strategy) and the force (level of investment) that will be devoted to the effort.

There are essentially three directional growth paths from which you must choose: growth, stability/maturity, and retrenchment. Each path corresponds with a major phase of every industry's product life cycle, and each has different financial demands and rewards.

Here are some questions that may help you identify the various stages of the industry/product life cycle:

In the business under consideration, is the number of competitors increasing or decreasing? The number of competitors typically increases during the growth stage and decreases during retrenchment.

Do you expect to have pricing power? Price increases are often easier during growth and almost impossible during maturity and retrenchment.

Entry also becomes more difficult as established firms build barriers in the late growth and maturity stages.

Fast-growing product lines are typically profitable but have high investment requirements. As the products and markets mature, profits continue, investment requirements diminish, and the business generates cash.

During retrenchment, profits fall, the business continues to generate cash but at a reduced rate, and additional investment becomes less and less attractive. At some point, you will need to harvest the business to recover as much of the invested capital as possible by withholding or reducing investment, liquidation, or divestment.

Here are three things to remember when setting goals and objectives and using the industry/product life cycle to improve strategic decisions:

Start by setting feasible goals: Goals must be appropriate for the return potential of the chosen business. If they are not, one or the other must change.

Be aware of industry characteristics: Before implementing a new strategy, consider what makes sense for the business, given the stage of the industry/product life cycle. This consideration will help you choose the appropriate directional growth path for your business.

Aim high: Organizations rarely exceed their expectations. Plan for breakthroughs and they will be more likely to occur.

"Competing in the wrong industry at the wrong time is inviting defeat."

102

Strategize

After selecting the business, setting goals, and determining the directional growth path, the next step is to develop strategies to achieve the desired objectives.

Competitive strategy is about acquiring and sustaining an advantage over competitors in the industry through performing differently in some meaningful way. Michael Porter, of the Harvard Business School, has identified three generic paths to achieving competitive advantage:

- *Overall cost leadership:* no competitor across the industry can offer an equivalent product or service at a lower cost.
- *Differentiation:* a company differentiates its offerings in some way that is meaningful to the customers.
- *Focus:* achieve low cost and/or differentiation for a narrow market, group of customers, or segment of the product line.

These three generic strategies are not necessarily mutually exclusive, but most firms find it difficult to pursue even one successfully.

Strategy sets the direction for the business: its goal should be to maintain or develop a sustainable advantage over competitors. In developing your strategy, consider the information gathered and analyses performed in the previous steps. You will need to articulate the attributes of your products or services, which should be aligned with the needs and/or the desires of the customers. The accompanying pricing strategy must be predicated on both costs and competition. Define the marketing strategy further by identifying geographic, market, distribution, and promotional strategy decisions.

The outcome should be the definition of a defensible competitive position—either different enough that competitors will not challenge it or built on an advantage that is sustainable.

Here are some examples: offering the lowest-priced product in a market (overall cost leadership); providing products or services that are best-in-class on a dimension valued by your customers (differentiation); and delivering a product or a service to a specific, limited customer group or market, such as one defined by geographic area, or concentrating on one part of the product line (focus or *niche*). A best-cost provider strategy combines low cost and

differentiation to deliver value and achieve a unique competitive position.

The practical goal of a strategy is to provide customers with a product or service in a manner such that no competitor can deliver an equivalent or superior product or service at a lower cost in the markets chosen.

Here are three tips for crafting strategies:

Base your strategies on some source of competitive advantage: That's the key to success. Generic sources include low cost, differentiation, and focus.

Consider the relationship between competitive advantage and the industry life cycle: The skills needed to build competitive advantage change as generations of products move through the industry life cycle.

Don't ignore the importance of functional competencies and resources: You must align the functional strategies with the business strategies. Do not assume that functional competencies or resources are adequate to support a given strategy. Before launching a new strategy, assess your capabilities and needs.

"Strategy formulation gives you direction. Think of your travels as just beginning."

103

Set Priorities

S*trategic initiatives* are specific activities intended to address the big-picture issues and close the gap between the current state and the desired future state. They may be aimed at taking advantage of opportunities or solving problems.

Strategic initiatives are imperative when your firm faces a performance gap. Gaps appear when performance projections with current strategies are not likely to meet management and shareholder expectations. The gaps point to issues that call for adjusting current strategies, adopting new strategies, or both. Before creating initiatives, you must first identify and set priorities for the strategic issues that need to be addressed. Each major strategic issue may require one or more initiatives.

Strategic initiatives are often aimed at solving problems or making major strides toward implementing a new strategy. If you are addressing a shortcoming, try to determine if the problem can be

turned into an opportunity. Sometimes merely solving a problem will not make a business successful. In many situations, success lies in identifying and exploiting opportunities through carefully crafted strategic initiatives.

To be effective, you should identify strategic issues, develop initiatives for each, and set priorities for the order of those initiatives. A business seldom has enough resources to take on all of its high-impact strategic issues at any given time.

To make these determinations, you must answer two contextual questions. How much time do you have to respond? A critical window of opportunity or looming deadline will create a sense of urgency that determines time frames. Is there a critical path? Strategic issues may have to be addressed in a certain sequence.

Even if you must persevere to find the required resources or if you must purchase expertise outside the firm, you must take positive action to effect the desired strategic change. Each strategic initiative may require a number of separate, supporting proposals. Simple initiatives may not require elaborate planning, but as issues become more complex, comprehensive action plans or even project management will be necessary.

Here are three suggestions for dealing with strategic issues and initiatives:

Do not assume that your firm has the capability of seizing an opportunity: No firm has the financial, technological, and human resources to benefit from every opportunity. Opportunism without capability is a recipe for failure.

Be alert to possible showstoppers: When dealing with strategic issues, order and trade-offs do matter. If an offer to purchase your company arrives unexpectedly, for example, it's a strategic issue that immediately preempts all others.

Consider timing: Time pressures often limit the amount of information that can be gathered to analyze strategic issues. Unfortunately, waiting too long to react can be just as disastrous as moving too quickly.

"The most important issues must be attacked first."

104

Pursue Your Purpose

The holding company strategic plan articulates the purpose of the business and sets its direction. It must be consistent with the previously discussed statements of mission, vision, and values that form the basis for all lower-level decision making. We review these briefly here.

The mission articulates the purpose of the organization. A holding company encompasses a portfolio of businesses. Its purpose or mission sets out the types of businesses in which it aims to engage and the interrelationships of the businesses. A portfolio can range from a group of businesses focused on a particular industry, production methodology, type of customer, or other commonality to a group of diversified companies with little in common and virtually no interaction.

The vision describes the long-term direction. A holding company evolves or changes primarily by making acquisitions and divestitures and through

427

the changing performance of its holdings, so its vision may be described in terms of the number, size, and types of subsidiary companies it pursues, creates, or divests.

Values define traits of individual employees or the organization as a whole.

The holding company boundaries are established by policies. One major policy for a holding company is its degree of centralization, defining or limiting the activities to be conducted within the holding company and the activities to be conducted in the subsidiary businesses. Other policies may address the systems for allocating capital, pension plans, transfer prices, or market boundaries among business units.

The holding company must prepare a strategic plan. That plan begins with its goals and objectives, which invariably include expectations for the growth in revenues and earnings, cash flow, and the return on shareholder equity (ROE).

The strategic plan also should specify in some way the degree of diversification intended for the portfolio of businesses and the degree of centralization or decentralization of planning and control.

Finally, the plan should address the approaches for allocating resources. It is implicit that the allocation of cash available from the common primary sources of reserves, operations, divestitures, and

debt provides deliberate direction for the firm's development.

Three things to remember to do when formulating and implementing holding company strategies are:

Develop and implement strategies appropriate to the level, mission, vision, and values: Most holding company strategies are unique to that level. Holding company strategies deal primarily with meeting portfolio management objectives and rarely address competitive business strategies.

Keep in mind the purpose of the company: Holding company executives may be bankers in disguise. Managing the corporate balance sheet and reallocating capital to take advantage of the best opportunities is a key job of holding company executives.

Be practical with resources: In the end, the holding company is an overhead expense. The holding company head count should be kept very small relative to that of the rest of the firm. The corporate office does not produce revenue but may create considerable expense.

"The diversified, decentralized company has replaced the conglomerate of earlier years."

105
Follow Your Mission

Business units or subsidiaries of holding companies follow steps nearly identical to those taken by independent, focused businesses when developing strategies and strategic plans.

The strategic plan for a business unit or independent business is a high-level conceptual document that articulates the purpose of the business and sets its direction. It addresses creating and serving customers.

The mission statement of a business articulates its purpose and provides a guiding aim or intention. A business unit of a holding company may have its own mission statement, but all of its guiding principles should be consistent with those of the parent company.

The primary purpose of a business can be described in terms of whom it will serve, the types of products or services it will provide, and how, in general, it plans to meet the needs of the target cus-

tomers. Strategic clarity about the purpose of the business is critical because the purpose delineates what the company does and does not do.

The strategy statement of a business unit or focused business should specifically address how the business will win orders and satisfy the needs of its customers. Business-level strategies address the positioning of the business within its industry and typically include, in some form, the chosen generic competitive strategy: cost leadership, differentiation, or focus.

A business unit's strategic plan delineates its long-term direction and objectives. Broad strategic objectives describe what the business aspires to achieve or become. Those objectives should reflect the realities of the industry situation and the financial and human resources required to compete successfully. As with the corporate parent, financial goals should address growth, cash flow, and return on investment.

A strategic plan should include a definition of the skills or competencies that are critical to meeting the needs of customers and executing the strategy. Supporting functional strategies are intended to provide the requisite competencies necessary to implement chosen competitive strategies.

Strategic plans should describe important actions (tactics) to achieve the goals and objectives

and to identify and set priorities for the actions that must be taken to implement the strategies.

The strategic plan should also provide detail for the short-term (one year) projections of growth, strategic moves, and supporting tactics, along with management's best thoughts as to likely plans and developments over the next three to five years.

Three tips for formulating and implementing business level strategies are:

Think about winning orders in the marketplace: Consider why customers should and will choose your products over competing products.

Remember your position in the industry: Everything you do is within the context of the industry situation and relative to what your competitors are doing.

Use the strategic plan document as a communications piece: Communications play a key role in implementing strategy, and the strategic plan should be used for this purpose in your business.

"A focused business needs a strategic plan to communicate its objectives and strategies."

106

Write the Annual Plan

Congratulations! It is time to make things happen. The annual plan or budget is one of the basic vehicles through which strategies are executed. Every firm should produce an annual plan for the next calendar or fiscal year that documents the required resources in extreme detail, as well as the cost of implementing the new strategic initiatives.

The annual plan includes strategic, operating, and financial expectations for the coming year and is concerned with the coordination and control of internal flows of resources. It is the next step in refining the strategic plan and the business plan. The elements of an annual plan are:

■ The action plans for the initiatives intended to achieve strategic goals

■ A marketing/sales plan that projects volume sufficient to meet sales goals

- A volume/capacity plan that reconciles projected volumes with available capacity (plant, equipment, and labor)
- A capital budget that appropriates the funding for required equipment and other fixed assets
- An expense budget that projects the costs of the forecast volumes
- Financial statements (income statement, balance sheet, and cash flow statement) that establish financial expectations

These results will be compared with the goals of the parent company and/or the business unit.

Effective annual plans are integrated into the strategic management processes of the business. These processes include assessing the competitive environment and the firm's strengths and weaknesses and identifying the actions required to position the company. These management processes link the annual plan to the business plan and the strategic plan. A proposed, regular calendar for developing these plans follows:

- The first quarter is spent gathering information and assessing the situation.
- Second-quarter efforts include identifying issues, formulating strategies, and writing the strategic plan.
- The third quarter is the time to refine the strategic plan and develop the business plan, placing

special emphasis on the capital plan, which addresses the investment base of the business.

■ The fourth quarter is the time to write the annual plan for the coming year.

Here are three things to remember when building your annual plan:

Let the budget be a result of the planning process: If you start with a budget, it will act as a constraint on strategic planning. Let the benefits of implementing the strategic plans justify the budget.

Put control and accountability into the annual plan: Each strategic initiative should have a specific time frame for completion. Include financial and operational milestones so management can monitor the implementation progress.

Involve all levels of management in your annual planning cycle: Managers at the corporate, business, and functional levels must reach agreement on various aspects of strategic initiatives as they move through the annual planning process. Choices should be made with an eye to corporate or business objectives and market realities.

"An annual plan specifies the actions required to implement your strategies one year at a time."

107

Obtain Commitment

Successful implementation hinges on widespread understanding of the strategy. As a result, you must ensure that your strategy is clearly communicated to all employees. This communication must not be a onetime, front-end exercise; it must be an ongoing activity that is an essential component of your implementation effort.

When strategies propose major changes, leaders must be prepared for resistance. People resist change for a variety of reasons, some rational and some emotional. Often, comfort with the status quo causes many people to feel threatened by any substantial change. For some, though, resistance might be rooted in the realization that they may not benefit personally from the proposed changes.

Your communication of the strategic plans must explain their aims and initiatives, why they are necessary, and what impact they will have on the organization. When there are conflicts of interest or the

potential for some people involved to be hurt by the proposed changes, you should be straightforward. A leader should be trustworthy and demonstrate concern for all employees.

Commitment to the strategy is essential at all levels and must begin at the top. After achieving buy-in from senior executives, the strategic planning team should systematically roll out the message to everybody else throughout the organization. The members of the leadership team should be highly visible and demonstrate their commitment, individually and collectively, with consistent messages delivered in a variety of settings. The top managers should communicate to the middle managers and the middle managers should communicate to their staffs. Everyone should be included.

The most compelling way to communicate is in person and to groups small enough to permit interaction. Large group presentations can also be effective, particularly if they are supported by subsequent small group meetings. Some companies are enamored with expansive events. These occasions can be very symbolic and build enthusiasm, but they cannot be a substitute for substantive and interactive small group meetings.

Here are three suggestions to follow when planning to communicate strategies and foster commitment to making them succeed:

Involve people in your initiatives: That is the key to communication and commitment. Sustained involvement will foster cooperation, commitment, and enthusiasm. Involve employees at all levels in rolling out the strategy. The regular communication of progress in implementation will support and promote mutual commitment.

Communicate to achieve understanding: People can't implement what they don't understand. Understanding gives purpose and meaning to a person's work. Misunderstanding creates confusion and distrust. The goal is to communicate so clearly that you gain extraordinary commitment.

Bear in mind that opposition will happen: A new strategic initiative that alters long-standing routines and personal relationships will be resisted. Use communication to build an awareness of the need for change. Use informal meetings to neutralize rumors and speculation.

"People can't implement what they don't understand."

108
Align with Strategy

You have been getting the right people in place and communicating your plans to gain understanding and support. You must also take time to deliberately align your structure, systems, and culture with your strategy. Success is unlikely without this effort.

Begin with the organizational structure. Structures are typically depicted by organization charts that show managerial positions, lines of authority, and reporting responsibilities. Traditional structures are hierarchical, with a series of layers, and most use some variation of a functional organizational structure to increase efficiency by standardizing practices, allowing people to specialize, and centralizing decision making. As businesses grow, they may develop other organizing themes, such as products, markets, or geography.

Ensure that the structure matches the central aims of the strategy. It should allow for reasonable resolution of conflicts as well as implementation of

strong internal controls to set policies and goals, report results, and inform top managers. Delegation without effective controls amounts to abdication.

You should also align the organization's systems with the strategy. Make sure each system is structured to support the goals and objectives of your strategy. Key systems include:

- Communication systems
- Management information systems
- Planning and budgeting systems
- Human resources management systems

Pay special attention to the human resources systems, given the strategic importance of employees. Major elements of human resources management systems include:

- Recruiting and placement
- Development and training
- Performance measurement and evaluation
- Compensation, with special emphasis on incentives

Finally, you will want to align the culture with the new strategic plans. Positive cultures that value performance and focus on satisfying the customer will contribute to the success of the new strategic initiatives. Cultures that are divisive and focus on protecting the status quo or the interests of managers or employees will hinder the success of the new strategies.

The culture should embrace important attributes essential to implementing the strategy successfully. For example, a differentiation strategy emphasizing customer service should be supported by a culture valuing helpfulness and responsiveness to customer needs.

The following are three tips for getting alignment:

Let structure follow strategy: The organizational structure should facilitate, not inhibit, the strategy implementation effort. Structure should support strategy, not vice versa.

Encourage systems alignment through budgets and incentives: Use budgets to manage and control funds and emphasize investments that support the strategy. Tying incentives to key initiatives is a powerful technique for achieving alignment.

Understand that your culture counts: The organization's culture influences the employees to respond in specific ways when faced with challenges. Members of a performance-based culture will quickly synchronize efforts and find ways to support any new strategic initiative.

"Every system is perfectly designed to produce the results you are getting. If you want different results you probably have to change the system."

109

Work Across Functions

Specialization by function is necessary for effective general management. The major functions typically include:

- Marketing and sales—Creates demand
- Engineering/R&D—Provides product leadership
- Operations—Delivers goods and services to match demand
- Human resources—Attracts and retains the right people
- Finance—Funds the business and provides control

The functional managers must understand the corporate and business strategies, estimate the resources and capabilities required for their accomplishment, and then compare these requirements with current capacities. Functional managers should also set functional goals, which should be specific and within their control.

The challenge that all firms face is to coordinate the activities of functional units to achieve common goals and keep them from operating as independent or competing "silos." A culture of collaboration and shared values facilitates such coordination.

Functional strategies should be developed to describe how each functional area will support the business strategy. There should be a logical linkage from the needs of customers to business strategies to effective functional strategies and strategic alignment across the functions.

The derivation of functional strategies produces a list of issues that must be addressed in order for the functional areas to meet their goals. These issues then must be translated into specific, manageable actions. Action plans should include:

- Milestones (interim goals)
- Budgets
- Timetables
- Assigned responsibilities

In summary, these action plans define who is going to do what, by when, within specified budgets.

To integrate the action plans, group the functional plans by topic. When more than one function must work on a topic, they must plan their efforts jointly to avoid redundancies and conflicts. If problems surface, top managers must intervene and provide leadership to create the necessary cooperation.

Here are three things to remember as you work to achieve cross-functional integration:

Ensure that the functional managers understand how the strategic initiatives support the strategies: The implementation of any new strategic initiative will require some adjustment in the functional areas. If functional managers and their employees fail to consider the big picture, the result will be inadequate or conflicting support.

Use cross-functional teams to implement new strategic initiatives: With a skilled leader, these teams can be a source of efficiency and creativity. The teams must have the authority to make any necessary changes.

Reduce conflict by rotating managers through different functional areas: Zeal for one's specialty and the natural tendency to seek efficiency for one's home function can cause conflict on cross-functional teams. Having team members with experience in various functional areas will enhance cooperation and contribute to the development of the next generation of general managers.

"The functional units must work in concert to produce the desired results."

110
Execute with Discipline

Carefully crafted strategic initiatives and plans are of little value until they are executed successfully. Effective execution requires the right people to do the right things consistently.

A good multiyear history of solid performance consists of multiple individual years of successful results. The same holds true for failure: most firms that fail do so gradually, rather than in one catastrophic moment. Discipline and dedication are required to ensure successful strategy implementation and sound performance.

A firm's leaders must model the traits of discipline and dedication. Leaders establish standards for the employees and set the true tone for the culture, regardless of what is posted on the wall or written in the annual report. Thus, discipline and dedication should be attributes of the right people.

Your human resources function should reinforce disciplined action and dedication through its

systems of evaluation, rewards, and promotion. Many firms find that individual progress reports are useful tools in reinforcing discipline. These reports might simply ask each employee what he or she did during the current period (often one or two weeks) and what is planned for the next period.

Planning and budgeting reports are more formalized and often quantitative progress reports at the group level. They should be produced at frequent and consistent intervals and their results should be communicated to the appropriate managers. Workers should be aware of the state of the organization, so they can be part of the solution when problems arise and take pride in their efforts when goals are achieved.

Project management is also an important technique for implementing strategic initiatives with the discipline to stay on budget and meet schedules. It is essential to break complex projects into manageable action steps that identify a critical path and to track progress against the plan.

Here are three tips that will help you with executing your strategy:

Act consistently and consistently act: Execution is about attention to detail, budgets, and deadlines. Mistakes will be made and compromises will be required. Deliberate and sustained effort will ultimately ensure the best chances for your strategy.

Link the organizational reward system and strategy execution: The reward system of a firm focuses on and influences both individual and group behaviors. Good execution depends on a reward system that signals what is desired. Highly motivated employees will drastically improve the chances of successful execution.

Foster an open and supportive organizational culture: The individuals involved in executing a new strategy must feel free to question supporting activities. Both successes and failures need to be understood so that requisite new skills and systems can be developed to support the strategic initiatives being implemented or so that the initiatives may be revised to allow successful implementation.

"History has belonged to those who execute best; strategies can be readily copied."

111

Monitor and Improve

The results of a business should be monitored to determine if strategic initiatives are being implemented on schedule and within budgeted resources. A firm's environment and competitive situation should also be monitored to ensure that strategies and initiatives remain logical and to identify emerging or pressing opportunities and threats.

To execute strategies, employees must maintain control of the activities that are their responsibilities. Rapid feedback regarding results is a powerful motivator to fully assume responsibility, achieve goals, and improve performance. An associated challenge, though, is setting up data-collection systems that are accurate and cost-effective in providing the necessary feedback.

The best data-collection systems capture performance at the time it occurs, use effective coding systems to describe the events of interest, and label the performance data for efficient analysis. Those who

are managing the strategy implementation effort need the data in reasonable time so they can react appropriately. Data should be collected both internally from operations and externally from customers and the industry.

A review of current data allows employees to compare actual performance against their standards or goals. This comparison should reveal deviations from or exceptions to plans and, if substantial, prompt investigations.

A review of data accumulated over time enables managers to detect trends and extrapolate future results. Historic data are particularly valuable for leading indicators, such as incoming sales orders and backlogs, which are likely predictors of future demand. Trends in the economy and competitive environment are similarly useful.

If the data indicate problems, managers should strive to understand the underlying causes and correct them or adapt to them as quickly as possible. When data signify strong performance, managers should also aim to understand causes and to praise and reward those responsible to reinforce their positive behaviors and attitudes.

Here are three ideas to help you monitor, evaluate, and react:

Monitor for success, not control: The purpose of monitoring is to minimize the effects of poor per-

formance and maximize the benefits of good performance. The key to achieving these goals is to provide feedback so employees can anticipate problems and opportunities and better perform their jobs.

Keep your eye on the strategic prize: Don't let the monitoring and evaluation efforts focus attention on short-term setbacks to the neglect of the essential strategy implementation effort. A good control system should encourage adaptability and creativity rather than punish shortcomings or require inflexible commitment to predetermined milestones.

Monitor selectively: You can't monitor everything, so select metrics that both matter and give early warning of variations from plans and assumptions. What you monitor signals what you consider to be important, so choose metrics wisely. Be open to new information; emergent trends can be as important as deliberate plans.

"You can't manage what you don't measure."

112

Learn, Change, and Institutionalize

Our global business environment is constantly changing at a rapid pace. To survive, businesses must learn and change. No ultimate strategic weapon lasts long in business. Strategies are readily copied and even patents eventually expire.

Planning and implementing strategies provide opportunities for institutional learning. Such learning requires posing probing questions that challenge the status quo and seek new information. In order to formulate new strategies, you must evaluate and question your past experiences and current practices, as well as investigate industry and societal trends. The continuous cycle of planning, implementing, and evaluating strategies leads to learning and subsequent change.

The perpetual process laid out in this section describes one general approach to this cycle. You should adapt it to your firm, institutionalize it, and constantly improve it through learning. The value of

learning is that knowledge builds on itself. Continuous learning is thus the foundation of continuous improvement.

The ways of learning include experience, observation, research, scanning, and monitoring. The sources of insight include your own operations and employees, customers, suppliers, competitors, and society.

With the appropriate structure, systems, and culture in place, the transfer of learning will take place routinely within your business. This transfer will drive much of the change in your organization as you do things differently because you have learned what must be done and how to do it better. Change occurs most readily in a culture of intellectual curiosity and discipline, one with an emphasis on experimenting as well as producing results.

Leaders must take an active role in managing change in their organizations. Large-scale change can take years and requires patience without concession. Day-to-day change also requires a consistent effort. It bears repeating that leaders set the true tone for the culture and standards for employees. If they do not model change individually and collectively, no one will change.

Here are three suggestions to help you institutionalize learning:

Recognize that a learning culture is an organization's key to the future: Insights into markets gener-

ate important understanding of strategic opportunities. A learning culture that fosters curiosity will improve your chances of discovering the next big opportunity.

Understand and accept that learning is about change: Build a sense of urgency for learning by openly discussing the risks of not changing. Create time for learning, reflecting, sharing information, and building trust.

Make learning one of your competitive advantages: Institutionalize debate, allow criticism, and tolerate failure. Learn to face reality through unbiased lenses—or a competitor will force you to do so.

The steps that we have discussed in this section provide a framework for planning and executing strategy. The process, though, is a never-ending cycle. Constantly changing environments, customers, competitors, and employees require strategic management to be an ongoing process, institutionalized within the organization, executed with discipline, and built on learning.

"Produce and compete or perish."
—Thomas Timings Holme

Index

About the Authors

John H. Zenger, D.B.A., is the CEO and cofounder of Zenger/Folkman, a firm that employs evidence-based, positive methods to strengthen organizations and those who lead them. In 1994 he was inducted into the Human Resource Development Hall of Fame. He is the author or coauthor of seven books on leadership and teams and is considered one of the most authoritative voices on improving organizational performance and developing leadership.

A former television talk show host and producer for CBS, **Anne Bruce** has been a featured presenter for the White House, the Harvard and Stanford law schools, and the London Institute of Management. Her motivational programs on leadership, customer service, the power of human potential, and an array of communications topics have been featured at worldwide business conferences, at professional asociations, and in hundreds of corporations,

including Coca-Cola, Sprint, Ben & Jerry's, Southwest Airlines, The Southern Company, Lanier Worldwide, Blue Cross/Blue Shield, Paine Webber, Baylor University Medical Center, the American Red Cross, and the Conference Board of Europe.

John L. Colley, Jr., D.B.A., is the Almand R. Coleman Professor of Business Administration at the Darden School, where he teaches courses in corporate strategy, corporate governance, and general management. He has served as chief of operations for the Hughes Aircraft Company and as a director for numerous corporations.

Jacqueline L. Doyle, Ph.D., is Visiting Assistant Professor of Business Administration and former General Motors Post Doctoral Fellow at the Darden School, where she teaches M.B.A. and executive education courses in corporate strategy and operations management. She has consulted with a variety of U.S. businesses in the areas of strategy and productivity improvement.

Joseph Folkman, Ph.D., is the president and cofounder of Zenger/Folkman. He is a renowned expert in the field of survey design and data analysis. His passion to provide feedback and facilitate change is the source of his professional success. He is the author of four other books: *Turning Feedback*

into Change, *Making Feedback Work*, *Employee Surveys That Make a Difference*, and *The Power of Feedback*.

Dr. **Rick Kirschner** and Dr. **Rick Brinkman** are world-renowned professional speakers and trainers. They are the coauthors of the bestselling audio- and videotape series *How to Deal with Difficult People* and have authored six other audio and video training programs. Their book *Dealing with People You Can't Stand* is an international bestseller, now available in a revised second edition with translations in 15 languages. They wrote the entertaining and practical sequel, *Dealing with Relatives: Your Guide to Successful Family Relationships*, and they coauthored the book *Life by Design: Making Wise Choices in a Mixed Up World*. They now present their entertaining keynote speeches and training programs worldwide. Their client portfolio includes AT&T, Hewlett-Packard, the Inc. 500 Conference, Young Presidents Organization, the U.S. Army, and hundreds of other corporations, government agencies, medical conferences, educational groups, and professional associations.

Wallace Stettinius is Visiting Lecturer in Business Administration at the University of Virginia's Darden Graduate School of Business and Senior Executive Fellow at Virginia Commonwealth University. He

teaches M.B.A. and executive education courses in management, corporate governance, and executive development and has served as director of a number of publicly and privately held corporations as well as chairman and CEO of a NASDAQ company.

Morey Stettner is a writer and communication-skills consultant in Portsmouth, New Hampshire. He is the author of the Briefcase Book *Skills for New Managers* (McGraw-Hill, 2000), on which part of this book is based, as well as *The Art of Winning Conversation* (Prentice-Hall, 1995). A dynamic speaker and seminar leader, he has led hundreds of training programs across the United States on topics such as sales skills, public speaking, and effective listening. He graduated magna cum laude from Brown University.

D. Robley Wood, Jr., D.B.A., is professor and coordinator of the Strategic Management Area within the Department of Management at Virginia Commonwealth University. He has been engaged in teaching, research, and consulting related to all aspects of strategic management for more than 30 years. His research has appeared in such publications as the *Strategic Management Journal*, *Academy of Management Journal*, and *Long Range Planning*.